Selling with NLP

A down to earth examination of how NLP techniques can aid your selling…ethically.

Paul   Archer

High House Publishing

First published in Great Britain in 2016 by High House Publishing, High House, Priors Norton, Gloucestershire, GL2 9LS, United Kingdom.

Printed and bound in Great Britain by Lulu.com.

Copy edited by Angie Bruce

Cover designed by Vector Designs

ISBN 978-0-9933112-6-0 (Paperback)

ISBN 978-0-9933112-7-7 (eBook)

For all your sales training needs, in-house requirements, contact Paul at:

paul@paularcher.com
www.paularcher.com
www.sellingwithNLP.co.uk
+44 (0)1452 730276

This book is dedicated to my sales manager in 1996 who introduced me to NLP in selling and arranged for me to have extensive training to a Master Practitioner level by the year 2000 – Ian Carlton.

And all the salespeople I've trained Selling with NLP since then. Some of them knew it was NLP but for many I declined to say, preferring them to have an open mind first.

And all the customers and clients I've consulted and sold since then, exposing them to subtle NLP to smooth along the sale. I declined to say it was NLP as well.

But for you, you're ready; you're ethical…so I can say.

Table of Contents

Selling with NLP

NLP or Neuro Linguistic Programming is an enormous subject. It all began way back in the 1970s and because of its viral nature, has spawned into many hundreds of applications today. Originally created by Bandler and Grinder, these two guys mastered a technique for modelling or copying what people did well so they could then teach this to anyone who chooses to learn. Clever really, almost like a replication device you see on science fiction movies.

Way back 30 years ago, they used their new found technique to model psychiatrists and therapists and for many years focused on these areas of use for NLP.

However, all was not lost in the sales area. Richard Bandler began to watch excellent sellers and published some wonderful books on selling. They are slightly heavy and concentrate a lot on really subtle techniques. Tony Robbins rammed the subject into the mainstream and has taken sales applications to the next generation. Kerry Johnson is another good NLP and Sales author. His books are also worth a read.

The use of NLP in sales has matured recently and is being much more accepted by sales forces. I've coined the phrase Rapport Selling or Rapportselling and use this widely to describe techniques that help sales using NLP.

You know I'm a really big fan of NLP in sales. Of course you can get jabs for NLP at the chemists.

Let me explain.

The Connection with Selling

This book is dedicated to the sales professional and explores the NLP tools that can be used to help the salesperson sell more.

Come on, isn't that what sales is all about (even in this politically correct world)? These NLP tools will help you sell more of your product or service -- period.

NLP and the Sales Process

Before we dive into the various NLP tools we can use in selling, I wanted to wrap them around the typical sales process we all use. Firstly I'll NLP the standard sales process.

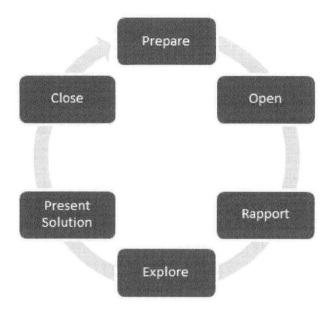

I know the customer is now in control of the buying, latest statistics show that in a typical business to business sale, the buyer is almost 60% into their process so the sale cycle above doesn't work as well as it used to. Typically the buyer has explored their options and is now looking to buy and wants you to present your solution immediately.

In business to consumer sales, customers want to handle the whole sale and buy your solution online. It depends on the gravity of the purchase of course, and there's still a place for face to face or virtual contact with a salesperson. In the future we'll see more and more automation with algorithms and automated intelligence doing much of the presenting of solutions. But that's in the future.

Today, when you secure the opportunity to actually sell, you need to be really good at it. And that's where NLP tools come in. They will ensure your selling is elegant, customer centric, relaxing and above all successful.

In the graphic on the next page, I've placed the typical sales cycle in the middle and around it you'll see the various NLP tools that are relevant in that part of the selling. Check back to the chapter index and you'll see them all.

Finally, promise me you'll only use these tools if you absolutely know in your heart of hearts that the product or service that you sell is the right one for the customer. Your ethics are congruent. Because I don't know whether they are or not, I've left the powerful topic of Hypnotic Selling, a branch of NLP, to my previously published book – Fluent Influencing – available from Amazon. But you mustn't open that book unless you're really sure.

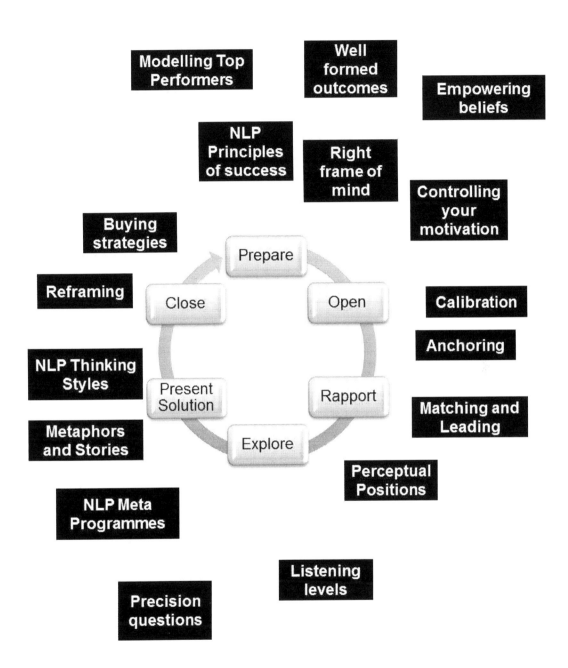

Mastering the Inner Game —Resilience Strategies

Your Inner Game Self-Questionnaire

We've got 12 questions for you to tackle right now as a self-assessment for how your Inner Game appears to you.

Rank each category from 1 (awful) to 5 (fantastic). Transfer your scores to the grid at the end to take a snapshot of your own view of your Inner Game.

Self Confidence - how good does it feel to be you? Do you have confidence and a good self-image?

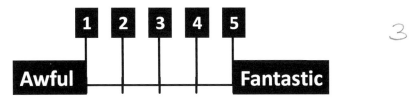

3

Belief in your product/service. Would you buy from your company if you were a prospect? Do you have an unwavering belief that your product or service can solve a problem for your customer?

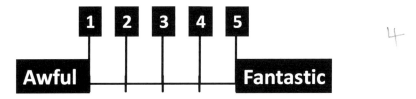

4

Belief in your business plan. Do you have a personal business plan in place that will get you effortlessly to your goals? If you don't, then put a low mark here.

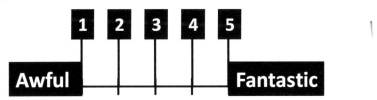

1

Conviction in the sales process. So many people have little belief in their sales process. Thus, they wander all over the place.

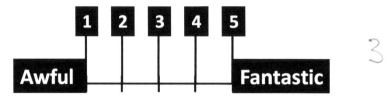

3

Inner beliefs about money. How confident are you about the thought of making money? We have programmes written from early in life around money (the making of and the talking about).

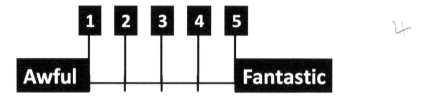

4

Belief in yourself as an asset. When you show up at a buyer's office, do you really believe that you are bringing value whether they buy something from you or not?

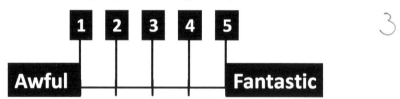

3

Ego management. Are you able to leave your ego at the door, or do you always need to be right?

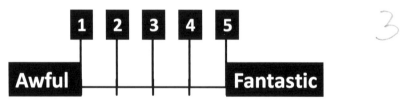

3

Detached from success or failure. Rank yourself low if you find yourself needy, desperate and attached to every piece of business, i.e. in famine.

3

Reason to sell. Rate yourself low if your intent is all wrapped up about you -- how much money you'll make and whether you can win the monthly award for sales. Rank yourself high if you're truly focused on the customer's problems.

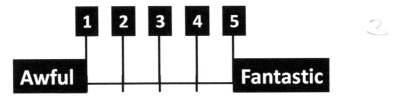

3

Feast. Rate yourself high if you believe that the market has enormous potential, whether any one person buys or not. (Be careful on this one. Some people rate themselves high and then get desperate in the sales cycle. If that's the case, you rank low for this one.)

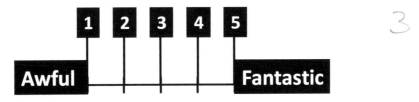

3

Positive or negative thoughts. Do you generally think positive thoughts or negative thoughts about your business life?

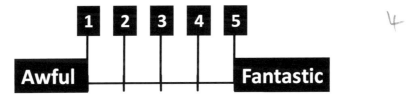

4

Compelling goals. How effective are your goals. I mean, how truly compelling are they?

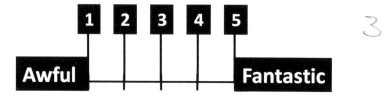

3

Self-marking

Pop your scores on the grids below to indicate your current Inner Game strengths and weaknesses.

Inner Game	1	2	3	4	5
Self Confidence			✓		
Belief in your product/service				✓	
Belief in your business plan			✓		
Conviction in the sales process			✓		
Inner beliefs about money				✓	
Belief in yourself as an asset			✓		
Ego management			✓		
Detached from success or failure			✓		
Reason to sell			✓		
Feast			✓		
Positive or negative thoughts				✓	
Compelling Goals			✓		

The 8 Commandments of Inner Game Mastery

Thou shalt...

1. Not let others dominate or control you
2. Not dwell on the past
3. Not try to attempt too much
4. Not own other people's problems
5. Forgive yourself whenever you make a mistake, it wasn't done on purpose
6. Merge with other people
7. Not try to please everyone all the time
8. Enjoy the present

Creating Compelling Outcomes

Achieving Compelling Outcomes

I'm sure you've heard the phrase "Compelling Outcomes". It stems from the study of Neuro Linguistic Programming (NLP) and turns the old topic of goal setting on its head.

The main premise is that traditional goal setting begins at the starting line and talks about setting the future direction. Since goal setting must start somewhere, let's continue to think of it in this manner, but where I'm coming from today is to see your goal from the position of actually achieving it.

Imagine that you have achieved your goal and that you are able to look back at the achievement process.

In this way, we're able to fully visualise achieving the goal, experience what it feels like, hear what success sounds like and make the whole goal far more compelling than it appeared when it was first written down on paper.

Future Pacing

The phrase "future pacing" rears its head here. It means taking your thoughts to a future event. I used to love doing this during my NLP training – closing my eyes and drifting along my timeline until I reached the event, dropping out of my timeline and slipping into a future event, really feeling that I was actually there.

It took some practice, but once you get over the "nerdy" element of hypnosis and imagining the future... then you're on a roll.

I enjoyed the time travel element and being able to let loose with my imagination. After all, it's my mind, and no one else knows what I'm doing.

Pacing Your Goals

One goal that I set in 1997 and vividly future paced came to fruition late in 2000. I can still vividly see the goal being achieved in my tiny office in my old house. It was a great feeling and proof that it really worked. So let me show you how it works and how it might just take your goal setting or compelling outcomes to a new level.

A great little acronym to help you in making your goals more compelling is PACES. It stands for:

- Positive
- Achievement
- Control
- Effect
- Step into the Future

Positive

Phrasing your goal in a negative sense can be self-defeating. Telling your brain not to do something is neither inspiring nor practical.

If I said to myself, "Don't put on any more weight, Paul", it would send my brain into spasms and I'd not get anywhere. In fact, the thought process would probably begin with thinking about gaining weight, because in order to consider not gaining weight, the subject of weight gain would, obviously, be my first thought. Thus, weight gain might actually be the first outcome.

Not good.

No, instead I phrase it as a positive forward sentence, such as "I need to get into shape".

It gives me something to aim for and something to strive towards.

Achievement

Many people talk about making their goals SMART. I'm sure you've heard of this before as it's been doing the rounds for decades now and is pretty clever or smart in its own right.

Specific, measurable, achievable, relevant and time bound. SMART works really well with business type objectives and I would definitely suggest you use it once you've broken your goal into bite-sized chunks.

But for meaningful and compelling outcomes, it doesn't work.

Instead, take yourself up into your timeline and whizz off into the future to a time when you have achieved it. Try to imagine the moment as vividly as you can. No, hold on, have you really got this timeline thing cracked?

First of all, ask yourself, "Where does my future point to?" For many people, it's straight ahead and slightly curved upwards to their right. This is the direction that most people look for their future thoughts, their imagination and their creativity. But you might be different – it doesn't really matter. Your true need is in knowing where your future timeline goes.

Now, imagine yourself whizzing along the timeline. Personally, I head up to the skies first and then zoom along the timeline. When I reach the moment, I stop, look down and there I am in the picture. I flow downwards and settle on the ground and can see myself quite clearly.

It's here that you need to see what it looks like to achieve the goal. What do you see around you, what do you hear, who else is there, what are you looking like, what expression do you have, where are you? Now step into your body like one of those 1950s alien movies where the baddies arrive on planet Earth and take over human bodies. Now you are yourself. How are you feeling, what's in your mind, what can you see?

I can imagine you might be feeling a little bit quirky, but if you do this well and practise it, you'll soon be able to know exactly what it's like to achieve the goal.

Control

Put simply, can you make the goal happen yourself? Are you in control or are you relying on someone else or something else to achieve it for you?

My goal is easy -- not to achieve, might I add -- but easy under this category, because I'm in control here, it's my self-motivation that's involved and not much else.

But your goal might not be down to you. For example, you might want to be able to motivate your sales team better. Fine. Your own skills can be improved in this area, but you also need the right team for them to be motivated. Some people are impossible to motivate.

Effect

What's the effect of achieving your goal on everyone around you? Does it fit your life and the people around you? For example, a goal to make £250,000 this year is fine, but working all the hours and never getting to see your family until Christmas night might not be in keeping with who you are.

My goal of getting into shape can be achieved because it fits who I am and what I'm about, but I need to be careful that I'm not always at the gym, ignoring my family and that I don't have special diet menus and eat at special times that keep me from enjoying family meals. That wouldn't be fair on my family or me.

Make sure the goal is in keeping.

Finally…

Step into the future

This is my favourite and I've already mentioned it a few times. Jump onto your timeline, whiz along it and find the moment when you've achieved it. Remember, you've already been there so going there again will be easy.

But this time, you need to slow down on your way back because I'm going to ask you to see what milestones you crossed as you achieved your goal. Have a look down to see what you're doing along the timeline and make a note of these because they'll become the action steps needed to achieve your goal.

For me, I can see speed walking with my dog, Brody, along the meadows during January and February at dusk. March, April and May sees me running along the meadows as it gets drier and lighter in the evening. In June and July, I start running in the wheat fields near our house in the paths made by the tractors as these become like running tracks. And finally, in August as we head out to France, I can see myself running along those gorgeous strips of sand in France.

Making Goals the Right Size

For most people, the fear of failure is the overriding concern that prevents them from making well-formed goals. One issue is that the goal may seem out of reach. A good example is that of a sales adviser who enters the financial services industry and wants to be the very best performer within 6 months.

The opposite is also true. A goal might seem trivial, and so not worth doing or may be relegated to the bottom of the list. Can you think of any examples? An adviser needing to sort through her paperwork, tidy the desk, write a report or make a phone call. We call this procrastination.

An answer that Neuro Linguistic Programming (NLP) gives is the idea of chunking up and chunking down.

Chunking up

When a goal is too small, simply ask yourself the question:

This steps the goal up to a higher level to reveal more compelling reasons for undertaking the tasks necessary to achieve the goal.

Chunking down

This is particularly useful when a goal seems frustratingly out of reach. Chunking down doesn't eliminate the original goal; it breaks it down into manageable chunks.

Ask yourself:

This question will throw up a number of problems. Take each problem in turn, and ask the same question.

This question will turn problems into smaller goals.

Stretching Your Goals

On the 8th May 2012, Dan Martin set off with his Speedos and a swimming cap to swim from Canada to France. Wow. But then he's going to get on a bike and cycle across Europe through Russia and over to Alaska. Crikey. Then he's going to run to New York. Absurd. An extreme athlete – his website's http://www.danmartinextreme.com

Talk about "bigging" up your goals... Dan has gone for one of the biggest goals known to man and good for him. But this got me thinking about goal setting for us mere mortals. Do we really challenge ourselves when setting our own goals and objectives?

For my 40th birthday my wife bought for me a three-hour excursion with a Police Traffic Officer in his excessively fast Volvo. Was I excited? The first lesson was how to control a car whilst skidding, then he taught us how to drive really fast. The finale of the lesson was to take the wheel of his hideously fast Volvo and drive as fast as I could along a public motorway. I tell you I was scared.

A friend of mine came along to keep me company and this was great as we could make mistakes together and not feel so bad. But to make a mistake when driving at more than 100mph on a public highway could be dangerous. Very dangerous. "You take the wheel first," said the policeman. "And take us as fast as you can, but don't forget what I taught you." Great advice, especially the negative, so my brain immediately forgot everything he taught me.

But I knew a little bit about setting goals so I said to myself that I would exceed 115mph. I knew my limits!

Off I went cruising at 70mph. "OK," said the policeman. "Let's take it up". And off I went 80... 90... 100mph... 110... 118mph. Was I thrilled! Safe and relieved, I slowed down and let my friend David have a go.

Within a minute he was doing 136mph. I asked him afterwards how he managed it. David said than after I'd gone first and he could see himself going faster than me, it was now easier.

So stretch your goals – you'll be amazed what you are capable of. Ten years ago, David Beckham was the only real master free-kick taker in the Premiership. He was so good they named a film after him, "Bend it like Beckham". Nowadays, every team has one or two specialist free-kick takers.

In May 1956, after years of training and dedication, Roger Bannister broke the 4-minute mile. Within the same year, another 37 people had done the same thing. And the following year, a whopping 300 people achieved the 4 minute mile.

So stretch your goals just that little bit more. Instead of focussing around 115mph, I should have targeted myself for 130. Just that little bit faster.

Goals Board

This idea to add extra testosterone to your goal setting is a little old hat now, but worth considering as it is quite remarkably effective.

In a similar manner, when you visualised your goals and imagined them being achieved, you represent this as a Goals Board. Up on a big white board or poster, create, draw, and cut 'n paste images or graphics that represent your goals. Keep the white board in view constantly and it also serves the purpose as an affirmation as well.

Here's an example:

Mental Rehearsal for Top Performance

I've always admired great film stars – Hollywood actors who just seem to be in such control -- so with-it. Arnold Schwarzenegger or Daniel Craig or Tom Hanks, they seem to be able to handle anything, achieve anything. But of course, it's only acting and a story. They're probably not like that in real life. Or are they?

So how do they get to be so confident? This is a useful strategy, so let me share with you how.

Have you ever watched the Olympic Games on TV and noted the sheer concentration of athletes at the top of their game as they count down the moments before their starting gun fires and they enter the most important race of their lives?

Watching really closely, you can see their eyes flicker and move around as though they're experiencing a movie in their heads, and indeed they are.

Ninety-nine percent of Olympians are rehearsing their race mentally as though they were running the competition of their life or swimming the 100 metres effortlessly and successfully.

Mental rehearsal has been known for years now to be a valuable way of preparing yourself for a major event. The Soviets used it for years back in the 1970s and we all thought their athletes were using illegal drugs. It's the act of running a motion picture through your mind of the actual event with you achieving great success, before the event has started. This is enough to trick the brain and floods your body with the positive states it needs to win. Apparently the brain finds it hard to distinguish real with imaginary if the made-up picture is vivid enough.

So the next time you've got something big coming up, such as a major sales meeting to run or a team motivation talk, and you're worrying too much or you just need an extra boost, try imagining a film in your head, with you the main star acting out the plot. You're the star of the show. You're also the director, the Steven Spielberg and you can control the way you act, the resources you have and the success you achieve. Keep the intrigue moving. This is not a photograph, but a wide-screen movie. Make it exciting and eventful. After all, it's your imagination and you don't have to tell anyone.

Trick your brain into believing it's real and come the big day, you'll be able to cope and perform in a way that you imagined. Go on, give it a go, try it, it works.

Funny the way Arnold Schwarzenegger became a Californian Governor, he acted the part so often, and he became the person. Spooky stuff this mental rehearsal.

Lanes and Lines Help You Appreciate Your Goals

Like a lot of men in their middle age I need to keep fit and keep the pounds off and up to now I've been running around the countryside that surrounds our house here in Gloucestershire, UK. But constant running can cause serious damage to your health, noticeably the knees.

So I took up lane swimming in our local baths. Swimming up and down the lanes for an hour, that way you don't bump into people or crash into the sides too often. Pretty boring but did you know you can get a gadget to listen to your iPod underwater – now that's cool.

Not the point I'm making today though.

Last week, the guys at the pool decided in their wisdom, not to put any lanes up, so we all swam as best we could. But what a nightmare. Swimmers were veering off to the side, I must have crashed into other people a dozen times, it slowed me down, I had to pause often to look up to see where I was going and it was terribly frustrating. It made the whole process far more thorny and arduous.

On my way home in the car that night, the light snow made it tricky to see the white lines in the middle of the road. The upshot was I slowed down, became more aware of the drive home and more cautious.

You see, having no lanes to swim in or lines to drive along is like operating without goals. To not have a clear, thought through direction to follow in your professional life, a mapped out plan to achieve your dreams and aims.

Picture the Outcome

Here's a simple question you can ask your client that will just ooze advantages for you both.

Deeply engrossed in his new Xbox 360 game Call of Duty 4, my son momentarily looked up at me when I entered his room. "What you up to son?"

"I'm shooting the baddies Dad, look I'm in the Blackhawk Helicopter, can you see me?"

Now is this is what the world is coming to?

Oddly enough it helps us enormously when we are selling or coaching people.

You see customers and coachees alike don't go for features or processes, they simply want to get a result from the activity, just like my son in his Blackhawk Helicopter. They want a result. They want an outcome that solves a problem they have or achieves a goal.

It does sound a bit simplistic but we should just ask them what this end goal or outcome is. And here's a neat little tip, ask them what it looks like with them in the picture.

More and more of us are increasingly visually based, so creating a picture in our head is very easy and if you can ask them to put themselves in that picture, you're onto a winner.

"What does your aim look like Michael? How does it appear with you in it?"

"Go on play a little, describe it to me?"

"I'm curious to know, what makes you want to do that?" Or "I'm really interested to know why you want to get to that end result, do you mind telling me?"

And bingo, you know what it looks like for them so you can tailor your sales message or coaching programme to their needs and you get into their world a little bit more to find out more of their values and reasons.

Simple questions but really valuable.

And I'd better get my son out into the real world a little more often. "Time to switch off the Xbox now Lewis!"

Sales Performance and Beliefs

How Beliefs Affect Sales Skills

Imagine or think back to a memory of a giant oak tree, one that's over a hundred years old. Visualise the tree now in high summer.

The branches in foliage, bright green and proud, moving slowly in the wind. The trunk creaking with the weight of the branches and below ground, stillness.

Below the earth lie the roots, enormous structures just below the surface and spreading uncontrollably. The root structure is enormous, and this old oak tree has roots double the size of what you see on the surface. The roots collect all the nutrients and goodness from the earth to feed the tree but what you see is only what appears at the surface, we don't see anything below ground.

This is how a person operates. Let me explain.

The twigs and foliage are the results the person is achieving, the thicker branches closer to the trunk are the behaviours which drive the results. The trunk itself is the person's skills and abilities. This is all we see when we encounter people.

Below the surface are the person's thinking and beliefs. Their beliefs and thoughts affect their skills which influence behaviour, which drives results.

But we can't see beliefs or someone's thoughts except in alien invasion Hollywood movies. No, these are hidden and totally influence what we see above the surface.

Change the beliefs and you'll alter skills and influence behaviour which will drive the results. Have negative beliefs about what you're doing and you'll behave negatively. Makes sense really.

You can train someone to increase their skills and knowledge, but you can't train their beliefs and if these remain negative, the training will often be wasted. It's all how someone feels about the process, not how they can do it.

How Do Beliefs Evolve?

Very early on in your life. When we're born, we're like a sponge and during the formative years of our life we soak up everything around us.

Our parents' views, teachers, siblings' views, the news and atmosphere, how you're treated, our friends, where we live, holidays. All this experience goes into our subconscious, our sponge. Everything we experience is soaked until the sponge can take no more and by then we've formed our views and cemented our beliefs.

It's these beliefs that will come back to haunt you when you are asked to cross sell by your employers.

The current generation entering the workforce, the Generation Ys, are filling up call centres and front line customer service positions. Mostly under 30, this generation is being asked to cross sell, so how do they react? What are their beliefs when it comes to selling and pushing products onto poor unsuspecting customers?

Of course everyone's different, but what's been in the news during their formative years?

Financial scandal after scandal, mis-selling, corporate problems, banking crises caused by drastic over lending, consumerism gone wrong, bank bashing and a general mistrust of salespeople.

So what do you think the current Generation Y think and believe about cross selling?

Interesting, isn't it, but walk into any large corporate call centre and the vast bulk of the teams are Generation Ys.

In over 35 years in the financial advising world, I've noticed three distinct limiting beliefs around closing, money and client types.

Closing

Or better put, helping the client to make a decision. The issue here is that none of us want to be pushy or "salesey" in the fee based world and that closing or heaven forbid, overcoming client reservations, can make us come over as an old fashioned life assurance salesperson that may have been trained in the 1980s or 1990s.

So our limiting belief is not to close or ask to go ahead or even to make a decision. Instead we let the client decide in their own time.

Now this is not at all bad, after all, if they're paying a fee for your advice, whether they decide or not is entirely up to them. We've made the recommendation and our highly capable staff will be able to process their instructions when they're ready.

The issue is compounded if it's fund based charging we're using, without a decision, then no charging occurs. If we want them to commit to ongoing advice charging, we have to help them make a decision.

What's the negative consequence of the client not making a decision or worse still, putting off a decision until a later date? It might be disastrous, the timing may not be right. Aside from that, we've taken time to arrive at a recommendation, huge amounts of research, weighing up the facts and emotions, taking counsel from others in the team. Our recommendations come with substance, so why shouldn't the customer decide? Our advice is correct, we've made sure of it and it's worth its weight in gold…so they ought to decide one way or another, putting it off is not a satisfactory conclusion for a professional relationship.

It's intrinsically wrong not to decide.

Money

This one comes down to our perception of money and value. It has numerous implications especially in the modern world of adviser charging. When all is said and done, it's down to how you value yourself and the advice you give. People are buying you; you're either comfortable with this or not.

Think back to your upbringing, your nurturing, how did you feel about money then?

For me, it all began when I was 12 and my first paper round which paid a princely weekly wage of which I spent every penny. I never had much money before that. I had a loving upbringing but we didn't have money swilling around the place in our post war council house. I left college in 1982 in the midst of a major recession, record unemployment and whole industries being decimated. As a Training Manager for a financial services firm in the 1990s, another recession bit hard and my expenses were routinely annihilated so my hotels became the budget varieties.

As a result, I value money, I value hard work and industry in return for a fair wage and I constantly have to secure my self-belief and confidence around money when I offer my fee schedule to clients! It's a lot of money, in my humble opinion. I need to focus on the value and result this fee provides.

But other people regard it as a paltry sum of money and don't think twice about securing the fee.

The answer is to grow comfortable with money since others view it differently to us. One person's £1,000 is another person's £1,000,000. It's all about value not cost.

Would you bend down to pick up a 10p piece on the High Street?

You're The Weakest Link, Goodbye

Money? Are you embarrassed about it? I heard a quote last week from TV presenter Anne Robinson, famous for "You're the Weakest Link, goodbye". She said "My best business decision is always to have been unembarrassed about negotiating a decent deal. Not being coy or shy about money is second nature to me."

I've always been coy around money, I'm sorry, it's me. I've always had to work hard for mine starting at age 12 when I trawled the streets of Weybridge, Surrey at 5am delivering newspapers. As a result, when I negotiate, I constantly google what others are being paid, looking at market pricing, but it's something I have to constantly work with.

What about you? Are you not shy about money?

If so you'll be a canny negotiator. But if you have hang ups about money, you'll never get yourself a decent win:win deal. Just ask Anne after all; "You're the Weakest Link, goodbye".

Four Strategies to Improve Your Beliefs

ROI

Return on Investment. For every cost there's always a return. Make sure you are crystal clear as to the value you provide. Calculate and estimate the return or the value that the client will accrue as a result of your advice.

Work out how much they might save or might not lose. Estimate the emotional value of the right advice, the peace of mind. Make sure you arrive at a figure that justifies the fee.

Make visible what's invisible

An enormous amount of work goes on behind the scenes in your role as well as mine. For you it's the back office team, the years you spend learning the ropes and studying for your exams, your CPD and all the articles, papers, trade magazines that you consume each week. The infrastructure, platforms, processes, software, computer algorithms that all ensure your client gets the right advice at the right time.

Ensure your client appreciates all of this and how it supports your performance and your fee.

Clients buy your uniform

Now I know you don't wear a uniform, so to speak. You play a role, a professional position in an established and reputable firm.

So when you're talking money with your client in the form of a fee, remember it's the uniform they're paying for, not you personally.

Let a third party sell you

We are the worst at selling ourselves. I'm a modest person; this is a value my parents instilled in me so to sell myself appears bragging or worse still, boasting.

No one likes a boastful soul. So find a way for a third party to sell you and justify your fee and the best third party is your other clients. The secret here is to master a client referral programme so all your new clients are referred or introduced to you by their friends or associates. Their friend is recommending you and justifying your fee.

The best introduction goes like this: "Give Paul a call, listen to his advice, do everything he tells you and pay him whatever he charges you" That's referral nirvana.

You're expensive but you're worth it.

Dealing with Clients

What kind of people are you comfortable with? Are you relaxed with rich people, extremely successful and fulfilled people or do they scare you? A rhetorical question but our client base that we choose to advise may well be richer than you, substantially better-off than you with wealth possibly inherited through the generations.

You may not have much in common with affluent people or think you don't , so you may not feel you deserve to advise them. You may have been educated at a State School; they might have attended public school and a Red Brick University.

Now you'll cope with this in varying ways. You might be ok with it, you might not, but if you hesitate a tiny bit, this will affect how you present yourself with high net worth clients and they'll sense it within 10 seconds.

Your limiting beliefs around who you should advise will affect your business levels especially if your client base's average wealth has increased over the years.

The trick, which I use myself, is to re-frame the situation. Re-framing is a particularly clever technique that literally changes the way we see something. Your client is not dealing with you because you play at the same golf club, they are working with you in partnership because they trust you, have faith in you, know that you are an expert worth paying for and if you get along and have rapport, more the better.

You are not their friend – that was a 1980s technique we taught you – that doesn't cut in the RDR world. They are paying for a professional financial adviser who can understand them, listen to their needs and goals, partner with them and provide substantiated and practical advice for them to act upon.

Eradicating Any Lingering Limiting Beliefs

I've spent some time with you discussing the three main limiting beliefs I've witnessed in financial adviser populations, and given you strategies to turn these into supporting beliefs about yourself and your capabilities.

Occasionally a dormant limiting belief might rear its ugly head; you need something up your sleeve to deal with these. When you spot one, ask yourself these questions:

1. What is your limiting belief?
2. Does this belief help you?
3. What examples can you think of when your limiting belief was not true or didn't apply?
4. How is this belief ridiculous or absurd?
5. What caused you to have this belief in the first place?
6. What's the consequence of having this belief?
7. If you keep this belief, what will it cost you in the future?
8. For whom is this belief not true?
9. Do top performing financial advisers have this belief?
10. How would you know if this belief were false?
11. What was the original purpose for having this belief?
12. What do you want to believe in instead?
13. What would be the advantage to you of having this new belief?

Have a coach ask you, your manager maybe, or a trusted friend. Or even coach yourself whilst walking the dog. Remember if your limiting beliefs, your silent killers of success, hold you back in one way or another, question the heck out of them to make you doubt them and rid them from your mind.

The Windscreen Washer Nightmare

We all know that how we feel affects how we perform and our performance in sales is much to do with what goes on in our heads and in what we believe.

Last month, I was travelling to a sales training event in Wales that I was running with pretty good internal feelings and self-talk. It was a beautiful summer's morning crossing the Severn

Bridge, I was on time, looking forward to the training, confident and enjoying the drive. Sun roof open, fresh air streaming through, I felt good…until the news came on the radio.

Legionnaires' disease was the main topic on the news. The latest research revealed that the most dangerous place to catch Legionnaires' disease wasn't hospitals or infected sky scrapers... but the car. Apparently the disease lives very happily in the windscreen washer bottle -- warm, still and the perfect place for the culture to grow. So all car drivers watch out, you could be in for a shock.

So how did I feel being about 1 metre from my windscreen bottle and having just sprayed the washer to clear bugs off the windscreen? And did I have the sun roof open to let in the water vapour? You bet I did.

You see, how we feel is all to do with our self-talk, and right then my self-talk wasn't worth printing and this made me feel low.

NLP Pre-Suppositions

So how can we control our beliefs and make them empowering, not limiting? Let's see what NLP has to offer with its pre-suppositions, which are the central principles of NLP. They are its guiding philosophy -- its 'beliefs'.

1. Respect for the other person's model of the world.
2. Behaviour and change are to be evaluated in terms of context, and ecology.
3. Resistance in a client is a sign of a lack of rapport.
4. People are not their behaviours. Accept the person; change the behaviour.
5. Everyone is doing the best they can with the resources they have available.
6. Calibrate on behaviour: The most important information about a person is that person's behaviour.
7. The map is not the territory.
8. You are in charge of your mind, and therefore, your results.
9. People have all the resources they need to succeed and to achieve their desired outcomes.
10. There is no failure, only feedback.
11. The meaning of communication is the response you get.
12. The Law of Requisite Variety: The system/person with the most flexibility of behaviour will control the system.

Famine or Feast. Which Sales Mentality Are You?

Margaret Thatcher, the UK's leader back in the 1980s, had her personal records released last month and one that hit the news was her diet plan. Intrigued, I started following the Maggie Thatcher diet and have been doing so for a week now. For those of you who have seen it, you know that you can lose 20 pounds in two weeks. It's all about feasting on protein rather than carbs.

Incredible stuff and we'll soon see how accurate the weight loss claims are.

The diet reminded me of the sales concept – famine and feast, which can help us all determine where we are placed in our Inner Game state of mind. It all depends on how we see things. Do you look out the window and see constant opportunities, believe totally in your abilities, feel relaxed and focus 100% on your customer's needs rather than yours? If the customer is not a fit and you don't get the sale, so be it; you move on to the next one knowing full well that you have the ability to solve their problems. You don't always have massive sales bubbling, you just know you will. If so, you're in a feast mentality.

If you stare out the car window and see scarcity and treat every prospect as a potential customer, thinking that you'd better win the sale at this afternoon's meeting or you're doomed. Are you constantly looking inwards at yourself, some self-doubt? Going from one sale to the next and continually wondering where the next piece of business is going to come from? Then you're in famine mode.

Of course, we all move from an attitude of feast to famine on a regular basis, sometimes hourly, but many salespeople I know are in the feast zone much of the time. On the other hand I know of salespeople that are in famine most of their working day. Constantly struggling and invariably blaming others for their misfortune. It's the government's fault or the customer was really awkward or worse still, it's back office support. Customers are never awkward, it's usually us (in famine frame of mind).

The key is to recognise which frame of mind you're in, catch yourself, and then do something to change. It's all how you see things and your state of mind.

```
DIET FOR TWO WEEKS ONLY

Abstain from everything not included in the diet and be sure to
eat what is assigned rather than do without.

NO EATING BETWEEN MEALS

BREAKFAST          Same every day
                   Grapefruit, 1 or 2 eggs, black coffee or clear tea

MONDAY      Lunch:   2 eggs, grapefruit
            Dinner:  2 eggs, combination salad, 1 piece dry
                     toast, grapefruit, coffee

TUESDAY     Lunch:   2 eggs, tomatoes, coffee
            Dinner:  Steak, tomatoes, cucumber, lettuce,
                     olives, coffee

WEDNESDAY   Lunch:   2 eggs, spinach, coffee
            Dinner:  2 lamb chops, celery, cucumber, tomatoes
                     tea,

THURSDAY    Lunch:   2 eggs, spinach, coffee
            Dinner:  2 eggs, cottage cheese, piece of dry
                     toast, cabbage.

FRIDAY      Lunch:   2 eggs, spinach, coffee
            Dinner:  Fish combination salad, dry toast,
                     grapefruit

SATURDAY    Lunch:   Fruit salad ( putin anything) as much as
                     you can eat
            Dinner:  Plenty of steak, celery, cucumber, tomatoes
                     coffee

SUNDAY      Lunch:   Chicken, tomatoes, carrots, cabbage,
                     grapefruit, coffee
            Dinner:  Cold chicken, tomatoes, grapefruit
```

Lady Thatcher's weekly diet sheet, with items crossed off, which she kept tucked into her diary, and a n

A Tale of Two Salespeople

Let me tell you a short story about two salespeople I knew in my real estate agency selling days back in the late 1980s.

Mark was just about to turn 21 and was a very successful and likeable negotiator. Mark was handsome, suave, bred to deal with very high net worth clients and oozed confidence and success. He was relaxed and measured. Nothing would frustrate him in the sales world and he approached his sales with easy confidence that he would be successful and provide copious value to his clients. He believed in a world of plenty, a bountiful sales mountain where, if he just showed up, he had the innate ability to do well. He just knew it. Never to show off, time for all people and an instinctive self-belief in himself.

Needless to say, he was the best sales negotiator the company had.

Tracy was the opposite. Always rushing around, never finishing things, constantly seeking re-assurance as to how she was doing. If she had a sales success which she often did, she would make sure we all knew about it. Not in an arrogant way, that wasn't Tracy, but in a desperate "look at me, I'm good at this" manner. Tracy was constantly looking at self-improvement books, always thinking she wasn't quite there yet, defensive of feedback. You walked on egg shells with Tracy, wary of saying anything about business. If times were lean, which they sometimes were, she would blame anyone or everyone. The recession, the banks, the clients, the government – there was always someone to blame.

Mark was in a mentality of feast; Tracy was in famine.

Recognise yourself yet?

Recognise anyone yet? Or yourself on occasions? I think we all have moments of famine thinking and times when we are viewing feast. Sometimes we say "I'm on a roll" which is totally legitimate because you've had some really good results which are spurring on your beliefs and attitude.

Being in feast is different – it's a constant mindset that you have even when your business results are appalling. You just know that so long as you carry on doing what you do, success will come.

Some people say they're on a downward spiral, which is often caused by a series of bad results, dismal luck and events going against us.

Famine thinking again is different, we persistently have the belief that we're not quite good enough, we have to hunt for every piece of business, everyone is a prospect, we hardly ever move out of our comfort zone and are constantly doubting ourselves.

A Checklist of Beliefs And Behaviours

Famine and feast are states of mind so let's talk about the beliefs and attitudes that we have when in these modes, the sales behaviours we perform and how our customers perceive us.

Feast beliefs

- Don't worry about rejection, they just move onto the next client
- Are confident of their own abilities
- Like themselves
- Generally have positive future thoughts
- Are relaxed
- Believe in showing up and just performing as always
- Are open to new ideas

- Have no need to prove themselves
- Believe in solving their customers' problems, not just selling them stuff
- Are confident of new business believing that the pie is big enough for all
- Believe it's not about me, it's about the customer

Famine beliefs

- Believe in protection first and foremost
- Think small, have limited goals and stay within their comfort zone
- Constantly think of themselves and their own needs
- Don't always like themselves
- Constantly have to improve themselves as they're never happy with their ability
- Fear the future and worry about up and coming events
- Fear new ideas
- Always asking for approval, asking "Am I doing OK?"

Feast sales behaviours

- Act relaxed, confident and naturally self-assured
- Plan easily and effortlessly both big goals and actions
- Stick to their plans
- Take risks
- Are internally motivated
- Look forwards rather than backwards
- Listen to their customers more as they put them at number one
- Really match their customers' needs and problems to their solutions
- Never get into an objection battle with customers
- Have meaningful conversations with clients, question and probe to solve the problem
- Are problem solvers

Famine sales behaviours

- Are external in their motivation – seek reassurance
- Try too hard
- Talk too much to put their points across
- Attempt to get acknowledgement from others

- Try to prove themselves too much
- Find it hard to plan, preferring to be continually flexible
- Worry about business and show this on their face
- Go into sales meetings desperate for the business
- Generate objections in their sales process and fight hard to overcome these
- Are rushed and busy all the time
- Don't take risks
- Act defensively when given feedback

There we have an overview of the main beliefs, values, behaviours and external aspects of the two types of salespeople mentality. Where do you find yourself? If you ever catch yourself, maybe fleetingly, in famine outlook, stop and take a breath and find a strategy to change.

There are a variety of strategies to become more resilient in your Inner Game. Belief change work, affirmations, examining your motivation, future pacing your goals, using success strategies from others e.g. Edison, positive attitude brewing, resource anchoring.

Yes, they all sound a little speculative but so is Margaret Thatcher's diet, but when you appreciate that your state of mind in selling affects 50% of your results, it's worth spending time developing your tactics to adjust your thinking.

Detachment is the Secret to Feast

I was at the football stadium last month having lunch in a rather pleasant restaurant. It was brand spanking new and the food, décor, surroundings appeared to be sumptuous. I was looking forward to lunch. Talk about aloof, the waitress might have well been an android, she was so detached to the process of serving myself and my colleagues, I thought she was talking to someone else.

We all meet people like this in customer service positions and to comment further is another article altogether. Personally I think you just need to employ nice people who just can't help being…well nice.

It would have been a more enjoyable experience if she had been more attached to our needs, shown some good communication skills and perhaps given a little smile. Maybe that was asking too much.

But I want to make another point though.

In sales we find ourselves sweeping from detachment to attachment. Our challenge is to remain detached from emotions but attached enough to connect and do the sale. The worst case scenario is to worry too much if customer says "no" – and not to take offence which many do.

If you put £1,000 of your monthly salary onto the favourite horse on the 3.15 at Kempton Park, then you'd be too attached to the race and would be desperate to win it. The prospect of not paying your mortgage would scare you.

However, if you just found the £1,000 and bet on the same horse, yes there would be emotions hanging on the race, but if the horse didn't come in, then your world wouldn't collapse around you.

The same in sales, we need to detach ourselves from the implications of not getting the deal. If you do this, mentally you feel free from the shackles, the stress, the worry of not achieving the sale and you'll enter a place of feast not famine.

The secret to the feast place, is to detach yourself enough to remove the anxiety that plagues desperate salespeople.

Don't detach yourself like my waitress friend earlier, but just enough to handle the Inner Game issue. Yes, back off when you feel you've become an irritation but no Mystery Shopper exercise has ever reported back that staff irritate customers and are too pushy. People who are too pushy are attached and desperate – don't go there.

So to be successful, natural, relaxed and persevere with a close…you must be detached, not aloof. Comfortable and connected but not desperate. Believe in yourself, your role and abilities and have a duty of care to all customers.

And not a selling skill involved as it's all in the head.

Selling Lessons from the Kennel Club

"You haven't, have you Paul?" "Yes we have" I replied. "We've 8 puppies and we're planning on selling 7 of them over the next month".

"You'll never sell them Paul, we had puppies last year and are still stuck with them all. Mark my words" was the warning.

I developed a sinking feeling in the pit of my stomach. How are we going to persuade 7 people to buy our puppies, there's no demand, we're in the middle of a recession. How would we cope with 8 puppies at home?

The next day we registered the puppies with the Kennel Club as they were pedigrees and you have to go through a strict process to adhere to their rules. As part of the agreement, you had to ensure that the puppies went to good homes, with fine owners who were going to treat them well, walk them daily and care for all their needs. We had a Kennel Club responsibility and had to prove that we'd done our due diligence on all the new owners.

This changed everything overnight. From wanting to sell the puppies keenly, we now wanted to find good owners for them all. From there on my wife started to interview prospective owners to see if they passed her "test of good ownership" and people became very enthusiastic to pass her test and become an owner of a Spinone puppy.

From being quite keen to sell, we became detached from the sale, the pressure had fallen away. This made the product more appealing to prospective owners and sure enough, in the first weekend, we sold 4 and the last 3 went quickly the following week.

What about you in selling? Are you too attached to your product or service? Are you too intense about selling, do you get a little too keen sometimes? Can you un-attach yourself a tad, take the pressure off and make your proposition more desirable.

Detaching yourself is the key to increasing the desirability of your product. Just ask Brodie's 8 puppies who all found gorgeous homes thanks to the Kennel Club rules.

Emotional Scars

All siblings fight don't they, especially brothers, and my brother and I were no exception. At one point I threw a garden fork at my brother like a spear and it sliced through the skin between his thumb and forefinger.

He showed it to me the other day to further enhance my guilt. He has a small piece of vulnerable skin.

Physical scars are a result of an injury to the body; emotional scars are a result of an injury to the mind or self-esteem. Same thing really.

Emotional scars are created by something happening in the past, which is then reinforced over the years to make it a scar. For example, your first job may have involved some negative feedback on your performance such as being awful on the phone prospecting for new business. Over the years, this is toughened with other events to produce an emotional scar.

So your sales manager asks you to start making more calls to drum up some new business. "Whoarr, hold on boss, I remember what happened last time I did that, I failed. I have history on that score, I can't do it".

An emotional scar has formed – a vulnerability and a damaged self-esteem.

Here's two ideas if you find yourself with an emotional scar.

Firstly, try to break the connection between the original event and now, the history. Tell yourself that now is different, stop beating yourself up.

Secondly, get a character with a halo to sit on your shoulder to offset the Gremlin on your other shoulder. The Gremlin is well aware of your emotional scars and will remind you of them and cement your negative feelings. Your Halo or Cheerleader will be empowered to contradict the Gremlin.

Let them ask you " Is it always the case that you fail at prospecting?" "Undeniably true?" "Has there ever been a time when you have been successful?"

That'll help you break the connection and heal the emotional scar.

I don't think my brother will let his scar heal, he relished last Christmas when he described to my three horrified children in vivid detail how his younger brother almost ended his life on that building site in 1969. Shame on you, Mr Archer.

Affirmations – How to Embed New Beliefs

Affirmations are really powerful little tricks that literally reprogramme the unconscious mind into believing something else. This is what you want to do. Write down on a piece of paper a short positive instruction such as: I am... or I will... or I always...

Then repeat the affirmation several times a day for 21 days. This sounds like a doctor's prescription. After 21 days the mind will be programmed to believe in the affirmation. Some affirmation rules:

1. Keep them short and in the present tense – I am, I will
2. Make them positive, i.e. to do something, not to stop something
3. Keep them personal to you
4. Only have 10 maximum at a time

I have a nifty piece of software that blinks my affirmations on my computer screen countless times a day. I don't see them as the blink is too quick but my unconscious mind is accepting them. This is called subliminal marketing and it was banned in the 1950s. So don't go doing this to your customers.

Try affirmations to embed your feast beliefs. They work.

Use Your Body

Many people now firmly believe that the body and the mind are connected. Put it differently, what you do with your body affects how you feel.

I like to go for a run, or to the gym or take the dog for a brisk walk. This gives me a boost of endorphins which make me feel energised.

A couple of years ago I spent an evening dressed as Santa Claus, all for good causes. Myself and a number of friends got together to work the housing estates in our town, to gather donations towards charities.

It was very cold, snowing and dark in Tewkesbury that night. But the magic of Christmas was in the air and we were all looking forward to a great evening of entertaining the children and people of our small town.

Being the last to turn up to the meeting rendezvous, I had been volunteered to be Santa that night and was given the uniform to wear. Long white beard, red hat, trousers and shirt with a big pillow underneath. I looked pretty cool I must say and with a "ho, ho, ho" I sounded the part too.

I sat on our makeshift sleigh which was being towed by one of the lads' 4x4s around the estate with carol music blaring out, it was a sight to behold and I was having the time of my life.

Kids were laughing, adults were donating and the evening was enchanted until…we arrived at the Acorns Old Peoples home.

My friend and I walked in together, he carrying the bucket of money, shaking it vigorously. We walked straight into the main rest room accompanied by the manager. Along the back wall were armchairs and sofas with a huge TV the centre of attention. There sat 14 old people slumped in their chairs, looking totally comatose. You could have cut the atmosphere with a knife.

I thought a big "ho, ho, ho" would do the trick so as loud as I could muster, I gave it a go. One or two looked around, but quickly settled back to the comfort of the TV show. My next trick was to move over to the window and beckon one of the guests over to have a look at the street scene. Laughing children, carols being played, Santa's sleigh and a trickle of snow falling from the sky. Wonderful.

And slowly one by one the guests began to leave their seats and look out of the window.

Within 2 minutes the whole atmosphere of the room changed. Yes, the scene outside helped, but the real reason was the body movements of the guests. Within two minutes everyone in that room was moving around energetically and it was this change in the use of their bodies that energised their minds and cleared the atmosphere.

So what do you do with your body whilst on the phone? Do you slump in your seat crunched forward, killing your diaphragm for hours on end?

Your posture can help you feel confident, energetic and in control. To do this when sitting, for example, keep your head up and maintain an open stance, both feet on the floor, square on to the desk, bottom to the back of the seat. This gives you a feeling of control over yourself and the situation.

Hunching your shoulders and drawing your body in on itself and angling away can make you sound disinterested.

Getting out of your seat occasionally and moving around. Standing to take calls also affects your mind and mood. Fresh air when you can, does wonders and sunshine in the winter helps with the mood swings. I've noticed call handlers with SAD lamps by their desks. SAD stands for Seasonal Affective Disorder and is mainly due to the lack of sunshine.

It's Your Fault, It's Your Thought

Mondays are always hectic especially the morning routine when you just seem to be late for everything. It was freezing cold that November morning and still pitch black outside when I learnt Bethan was having an inset day and wasn't going to school. So I became a baby sitter for my ten year old daughter, although I had stacks to do that day.

Bethan had the run of the house for the whole day. TV whenever she wanted it, laptops to play on, fridge was all hers and her two arch enemies – her two older brothers – were safely locked away in school. So I kept my office door open and listened out for her whenever I could. But she was fine.

My day was going very much to plan and the next item on my to do list was a run. I try to go for a run every day or so for 45 minutes, and since I was going to be working away for a few days this was to be the last run for a few days, so I really wanted to do it today.

How could I leave my daughter on her own at home? But my urge to run got the better of me, besides I run along the fields around my house so I was always available and I thought I'd take my phone just in case She'd be fine.

I promised Bethan I wouldn't be long and headed off for my run down the lane alongside the house, and turned right across a field right opposite my house. At the bottom of the field I normally stop to do a stretch or two on my aging muscles. From here I can clearly see the house. I looked up and saw, from a distance, Bethan at the front door, waving at me.

Or was she waving for me to return? Was she in trouble? Was she frightened and wanting me to come back home? Thoughts rushed through my mind. What have I done, poor Bethan she's in danger, what a terrible daddy I am. I must rush back and rescue her. So I sprinted as fast as my legs would take me.

Gasping for breath at the door I shouted to see if she was OK. "Of course I'm OK Daddy, I was just waving at you."

"But I thought you were in trouble so I came rushing back to see."

"Daddy, it's your fault," said Bethan, "It's your thought."

Later that day on my second attempt at a run, those words resonated with me. Bethan was spot on. It was totally my fault that I thought that way, I'm in control of my thoughts, no one else and I chose to think that she was in danger when she was harmlessly waving at me.

The Secret to Controlling Your Self-Talk

You see, we are in control of our thoughts, whether we realise it or not, so next time you're having negative destructive thoughts that serve no purpose, stop yourself, chuck them out, and control your thinking. That's the secret to controlling your self-talk.

The secret to controlling your self-talk is to analyse what you talk to yourself about, break it down and control it. Divide up your self-talk into two camps – things you talk about to yourself that are from the past and stuff you discuss with yourself that hasn't happened yet. Past thinking and future thinking.

Next decide whether the thinking was good or bad. Have a look at this graphic.

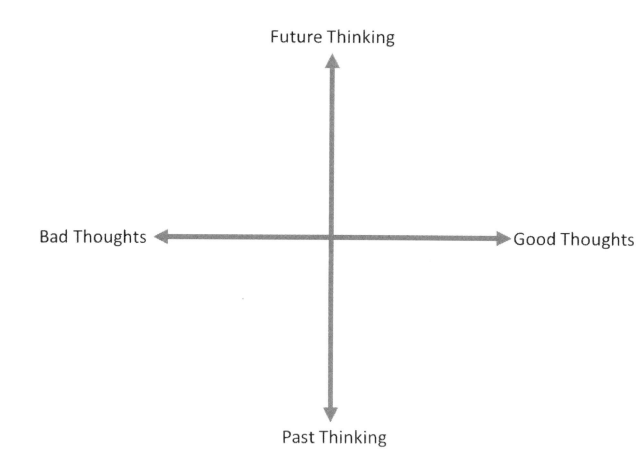

The Four Categories of Self-Talk

Now we've got four categories of self-talk:

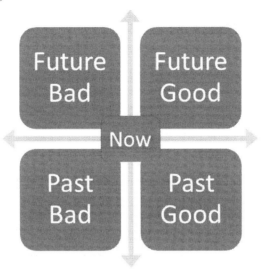

I've also added present thinking, for example "I need to slow down in this car right now".

So we now have five categories. Let's have a look at typical stuff we talk about that come in to these five categories:

Dangerous Past Thoughts

The plain fact is that if we get thoughts from the past too much, it serves little or no purpose. Yes some things are useful, for example I was asked a question from someone on my workshop about a previous encounter with a firm.

I was able to think back to the past and recount the story to help them understand something. I also had a fleeting thought about my daughter and that I wouldn't be seeing her until Saturday as she was on a mega sleepover. This was nice but kind of "I'll miss her".

The point is this. If we dwell on past good or past bad, it's not going to do us any favours. Yes, if we make a mistake, learn from it, then get over it. Put it on an imaginary piece of paper, screw it up and forget about it.

Future bad thinking is just as bad but also useful on occasions. I've got a big speech coming up next week and I've been thinking about this and making sure I'm very prepared and ready, so thinking about it has helped me prepare thoroughly. However, if I started worrying about it and stressing, that would make things unbearable in my head.

Of course there's always going to be an element of past bad thinking and future bad thinking but control it, don't let it dominate or control you. Spend most of your thinking focused on now and future good thinking and you'll not go far wrong in developing a positive attitude fuelled by useful thoughts.

Recommended Thinking

Here's my suggested proportions of thinking time:

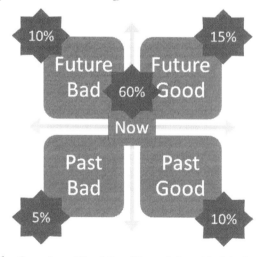

Focus on this and you'll do fine. Just like Man U tonight. Ah it's 9pm – time to go watch the football – I've been looking forward to this all day.

Wise Words to Handle Sales Pressure

How do you handle pressure in sales and sales management? It's one of the supreme causes of salesperson and manager burn out. Here's some wise words from a top performing salesman.

Once the rugby season finishes in April, my wife's face lights up and she hands me a list of jobs for me to do around the house and garden. The first Sunday was the turn of the strimmer. Unfortunately it happened to be the hottest day of the year and regrettably you have to dress for the occasion.

Boots, thick trousers, combat jacket, hat, safety glasses and rigger gloves protected me from the flying shrapnel of weeds, stinging nettles, grass, and other garden dangers which were being sent swirling through the air at rocket velocities.

I was sweating buckets underneath it all and must have lost pounds in weight…but I was protected and that was all that mattered. Strimmer shrapnel hurts a lot.

But how do you protect yourself from the pressure and stresses associated with your job?

Yesterday I was coaching a top salesman who happens to be the number one performer for his company. His greatest challenge is maintaining this position and handling the pressure put on him.

I was curious as to how he intended to handle the pressure, he replied "I'd rather be top and have to handle the pressure than be mediocre and have no attention on me at all."

A clever way of putting it.

But I was still inquisitive to see how he handled the pressure, because he obviously could. "What's the worst that can happen?" he began, "I ask myself what's the worst that can happen so I put the pressure into context. If something goes wrong, I have a bad meeting or I lose a deal, I'll put it to the back of my mind and deal with it another time. When I get home I put it to the back of my mind and say to myself - what's the worst thing if I leave it to tomorrow morning to deal with it? I just won't get down on it; mentally I'll not worry about it…what's the worst that can happen?"

"How do you handle the voices inside your head?" I asked.

"I guess I'm quite tough mentally and don't let the voices get me down. I know some of the guys get down with their voices but I guess I just stop them and ask myself to look at the positive side all the time…to move on and move forward."

The lesson from my sales friend: Look for the positive, learn how to park things, handle the self-talk. Easier said than done but it's important we all have strategies to protect ourselves when the going gets tough.

And if you ever want to let off some steam, get yourself a 50cc petrol driven strimmer that just wades through weeds and nettles. And with debris flying through the air, I just know that my boots, thick trousers, combat jacket, hat and safety glasses will protect me…what do you have to protect you from the debris that sales and management throws at you every day?

It's all in the Head

Today I've been helping some sales people learn how to pick up the phone and call new customers. Sounds pretty easy really but as soon I mentioned they were going to be phoning people who weren't expecting their call, they froze. You could visibly see the fear in their eyes.

You see, it's all in the head.

We know why this happens because we continually take calls from people trying to sell us something and most of us don't like it. It's only natural to want to be liked by people and to be welcomed. No one likes being snubbed at a party or ignored at a gathering and we've learnt from day 1 not to be a nuisance or annoy people. It doesn't get the right reaction.

Obvious really, so how do we get over this thinking when picking up the phone?

One way is to get it clear in our heads what calling new customers is all about. And more importantly, why are we doing it. So here are the five critical beliefs that people who phone new customers must have in their heads.

Your Customer Needs What You Have

Your customers do need whatever it is you or your company are selling. OK, if you're selling off the Yellow Pages, then you might find some resistance, actually quite a lot. If they don't buy from you then they will buy from someone else and that's not good because you have the product or service right here for them. Technology and data capturing these days has moved on a lot since the early days of grabbing the Yellow Pages and phoning everyone from page 1. At least you owe it to yourself to phone customers who do have a need.

You would buy from you

Do you like your product or service? If you were in the market for it, would you buy it from you? This is so important for your mindset. You need a belief that your product has plenty of value and is the best on the market. If you don't believe this, you won't give the right vibes on the call.

Your service oozes value

Your service offers value for money. Now value is different to cost, they are not the same thing. It's like nutrients and calories, they're just different but often confused. Value for money is a combination of benefits over cost, so if you don't see value in what you are selling, pump up the benefits. Convince yourself first.

You're good at this

You've just got to believe that you're good at this, you are clever, easy to get on with, reliable, trustworthy, you ooze integrity and transparency and you have the customer's best interests at heart. You must believe in this – you're good at using the phone and selling.

Laser your focus on what you're selling on the phone.

Laser your focus on exactly what it is you're selling to the customer over the phone and what the call to action is. Do you want them to call into your retail branch to talk further, do you want to go and see them, do you want them to buy something there and then? Be crystal clear what it is you're pushing on the phone and when you get talking, get to the point and get it done. The belief here is to know that there is a structure to use, no tricks, just structure and skills. Trust in your script and structure to get you results, not lady luck.

It's all in the head but as always it's easier said than done. But let's get done what's said and bring in more new customers to top up our sales funnel.

NLP Anchoring in Sales

Nautical term this is not. They are triggers that get your unconscious mind to leak a feeling back to your conscious mind. This affects your feelings. I'll go out later and be bombarded by images, sounds and smells that will bring back a memory. My unconscious mind will leak this memory back to my unconscious along with a feeling about the memory.

I could hear church bells and this might remind me of my wedding day and bring back those wonderful feelings I experienced on the day. I might smell some cut grass and be reminded of having to cut my own grass at home which is something I don't enjoy so will bring my state down. A tele-salesperson might pick up the phone to take a call and this memory might trigger a bad state. It could be that all morning he's had some terrible calls and he's conditioned his mind to convince himself that whenever he picks up the phone, it's bad news.

But anchoring can help you control your state of mind. The idea is to attach something to a memory so you can re-experience the feeling that is associated with the memory.

I imagine you've all heard of Pavlov's Dogs. A very famous example of dogs salivating with a ring of a bell because they associated the ring as the time when food gets delivered.

Advertisers spend millions on getting us to associate famous personalities with their product. I worked for a company recently that used June Whitfield in their advertising. There was June saying great things about the product and the viewers would watch the commercial, glance at June, get a warm feeling of security, nostalgia, integrity and then attach these feelings to the product being sold.

Very clever.

Our dog Brodie loves it when she's in the garden but loves it even more when she escapes into the church yard or next door to explore. Faced with a huge fence bill to ensure she didn't escape, we opted for one of these dog training devices as it was much cheaper and would create less turmoil. I was a little sceptical at first. After all, laying a wire underground around the boundary and strapping a collar on Brodie which would give her a short electric shock every time she crossed the boundary….well.

What can I say? And before everyone writes in to complain of animal cruelty, it didn't turn out like that. Yes she had a couple of shocks, but within a day she no longer approached the invisible boundary wire because she knew what might happen to her.

Within a week, we just put the collar on Brody and didn't even bother to switch on the electric current. We call it the "Oweee" collar and she has never escaped once. Now this is one big anchor and Brody relates the "Oweee" collar to pain on the boundary and won't go near there.

So we've produced a visible, vocal and physical touch anchor.

Now I'm not saying we should wear collars when selling, but what I am urging you to do is to set up your own series of anchors that will bring back a memory and flood your conscious mind with a feeling or two and this will affect your state.

A good friend of mine used to dread doing presentations until he went out and bought himself a special presentation suit. He self-talked, ran affirmations and did loads of mental rehearsal to ensure his presentation would be good when he wore the suit. He worked hard at this and he was good. So good in fact that he only needs to put on this suit to bring back all the wonderful feelings of confidence, assuredness, and the relaxed state he was in when he first wore the suit.

I imagine that he would only need to think of the suit. He could put a really good picture of himself in his mind's eye wearing the suit and presenting well and that would be enough to bring back the positive state of mind he needs to present. I wonder what would happen to my friend if he had to buy a new suit?

So how can you set up an anchor?

You need to experience the state of mind that you want to bottle up first. Now you can wait until this state naturally happens and make the most of the moment. Or you can go back in your mind's eye to remember a moment when you were going through that state of mind.

When you have the memory clear in your mind, really try and imagine it much more. Get in the picture; get in the zone as they say these days. Recall the sounds around you, the smells, the feelings and what you see around you.

Next put a stimulus into your conscious mind. Try and get all three senses i.e. visual, touch and sound. Go for taste and smell as well if you wish. For example you might press your right hand finger and thumb together, when recalling a favourite song in your head.

Repeat this as many times as you can. With Brodie it took a few "Oweee Collar" moments to anchor her. Just like our affirmations from earlier, you need to convince your unconscious mind through repetition. After a short while all you'll need to do is fire off the anchor you created to let your unconscious just flood your mind with those lovely feelings you stored up.

Try it, it does work.

So next time you're feeling low or negative or feeling that you can't sell anymore, get your body active in the right way, fire off some anchors and get that self-talk going to your advantage. Spend some time on your mind and remember that the unconscious mind delivers feelings but we can convince this to give us the right feelings.

After all, selling is a such a topsy turvy business. You have your ups and downs and we are only humans at the end of day. Flesh and blood bristling with emotions and feelings. Learn how to control them to give you that head start on everyone else.

Anchoring your Customer

Here's a neat little idea to boost your confidence and energy levels, and let's face it, we all need to do this sometimes.

We've all come across the term "anchoring" where we use a reminder or a trigger to recall something from the past. NLP or Neuro Linguistic Programming brings this to us and it helps us to relive past moments in our lives so we can collect the resource that we had in abundance at the time.

I have several anchors which I use to inject myself with a resource. For example, before a big presentation I recall a specific moment where I collect huge amounts of enthusiasm. If I want to relax I have an anchor that does just that. They're pretty much like speed dials on your phone; they just take you back to when you had that resource in abundance and trick the brain to feel the same way again. The more you fire up the anchor the more reactive it is.

Here's an idea when you want to help your customer to buy from you.

Take them back to a time when they bought something really successfully, get them to relive the moment, the emotions, the sights. Ask them to recall it in their mind's eye, describe it, why they made the purchase.

When they're really in the zone, anchor it with a sound, a physical gesture or a subtle touch on their elbow. As you approach the time for them to buy your product, bring back the sound or the gesture or do the touch.

I've used this whilst coaching. I've asked my coachee to think back to a time when they were self-sufficient, could handle anything themselves, were tremendously resourceful and action oriented. I usually anchor this with a change in my position – I use the catapult position where I lean back and put my hands behind my head and at the same time say the phrase "good for you". Later in our coaching session I might want them to take some action or be resourceful. I redo the catapult gesture, smile, say "Good for you" and wait.

It often works and they become resourceful and full of action plans, which is the goal of the coaching.

So try anchoring your customer or coachee next time and see if it makes a difference. And you can thank Neuro Linguistic Programming for that. But don't worry you can get tablets from the chemists for that.

Resource Anchoring

What's 15th Century Artillery got to do with having the right resources inside to do the job? Quite a lot actually, so let me explain.

Resources or states of mind are essential elements in our winning the Inner Game but to handle various situations competently, we don't just need skills but a certain state of mind. For example to do some coaching we need a patient state, an inquisitive and curious state of mind to coach properly. If we felt frustrated and rushed, then we'd probably listen to the coachee and then just rush in and tell them what to do. Not good.

It happened to me the other day, I was rushing around, constantly up against deadlines, when in walked my son Euan. "Dad, have you got a moment?" "Just two son, what can I do?"

"I've got some tricky homework on 15th Century Artillery."

"Tell me more Euan?" was my excellent coaching question and within 2 minutes I figured what he needed to do for his homework. "You need to concentrate on the power of gunpowder, Euan, and explain how the mechanical forms of artillery like the catapult were soon discarded in favour of the cannon which revolutionised siege warfare. Remember castles around the time and that they had no defence against cannons. "

A typical blokeish answer, yes we find warfare fascinating, well I do anyway.

But the point was, as a coach, I blew it. I told him what to do which is a cardinal sin. All because I had the wrong state of mind before I even started.

So what we need is a nifty little trick to exchange our state of mind at will and we have – it's called an anchor or resource anchoring.

An anchor is not a nautical term today, but a naturally occurring reminder of a state of mind. One of the most famous anchors known to the travel industry is the sick bag.

Just the sight of one of these is enough to turn a level headed and contained stomach to wrenching with pain and discomfort. So much so that the cabin crew don't even mention the sick bag anymore for fear of violently ill passengers.

What're your naturally occurring anchors?

All these memories bring back a state of mind because they take you back to a time when you first heard the music and tasted the food. The state of mind you had then comes flooding back into your insides and arms you with that state.

So how's this useful when selling or coaching people? A lot. Here's how it works.

Before you next go into a particular event, make a mental note of the kind of resource or state you need to perform well. For example, it might be a big audience presentation, a particularly tricky sales meeting or a difficult moment with your top performing salesperson. The big presentation needs confidence and self-assuredness.

Step One – recall a time when you had these emotions or states in abundance. Go on, think of a time now.

Steps Two and Three – whizz back into time and associate yourself with the event. Become the person again in your mind's eye, imagine you are there once again experiencing the moment. For anyone who's been to watch Toy Story 3D, you know what I mean by associating yourself.

Step Four – really imagine you're there and re-live the experience – concentrate on what you hear around you, can see, feel. Re-live the moment. Now this will allow the state of mind you had at the time to surge through your body, arming you with the resource needed to carry out a brilliant presentation.

Step Five – is some form of reminder or anchor as we call it. You might want to shortcut to this memory again in the future quickly. Just like a shortcut on your computer or speed-dial on your phone, you need an anchor to help you recall it again. Pressing a knuckle is a touch anchor. You could associate a tune to it or a strong visual – it doesn't matter, you choose.

Here's a little tip. As you wander through life, if you find yourself in a great moment oozing a precious resource, create an anchor there and then for use later on in your life. It's a useful technique.

I bet the creators of 15th century cannons anchored their experiences when they started pummelling castles to rubble with their new invention. That feeling of dominance and power was one to anchor. I wonder what a 15th century anchor looks like, feels like, sounds like?

The Secret of Smell in Sales

I'm going to share with you a neat way of always being in control of your state of mind. Imagine that. Being able to change your state of mind at will.

For those who know me well, you know that I love dogs. I have two dogs, mother and daughter, Spinones.

They're gun dogs. Bred to sniff out birds and game in the rough ground, disturb them for the guns to shoot and then retrieve the game for the gunner's pot later that evening. This breeding has been going on for centuries.

As a result, my two dogs have a masterful sense of smell; I've heard it's a thousand times better than ours. The thing about smell is that it has no barriers to recollect the memory.

Have you a favourite smell that just triggers the memory associated with it? Maybe a perfume smell that reminds you of your first love or the smell of freshly cut grass which brings back lazy hazy summer days.

Now that's the secret to managing your state of mind. Here's the strategy.

Make a note of the various states you need to perform optimally.

Maybe its patience, maybe positiveness, maybe curiosity.

Now think back to a time in the past where you had this state in abundance.

Relive the memory but this time try and associate a smell or taste. If you can, the mere whiff of this smell will transport you back to that time and inject you with the state that you had at the time.

Here are a few examples:

- For a relaxing, totally comfortable state – I smell sun tan lotion – this brings back memories of lying on the beach without a care in the world.
- Fresh cut grass helps me to inject myself with perseverance and finishing a boring job. As a teenager I earned most of my beer money cutting people's grass.
- To perform my best when in front of an audience I use saffron. This brings back memories of Iran when I had a standing ovation from an audience of over 200 people.
- For clarity I use the smell of cold air. This memory is when I walk the dogs early in the morning when it's fresh and chilled and the air smells wonderful. My head feels totally clear and I ooze clarity.

It works, it's worth trying, there's nothing to lose.

Subtle Anchoring

My audiences know that I move around the stage for a purpose, not randomly. I'll tell you more about this shortly because it's a clever influencing technique to move an audience to agree with your idea or proposal.

It's all to do with spatial anchoring – now that's another NLP term they took from the top drawer of dictionaries. Anchoring is merely a way to recall a state of mind from some kind of memory jog.

We've been doing this for centuries. The smell of grass floods back pleasant memories of working in people's gardens when I was a young teenager earning my first pay cheque. The smell makes me feel good. Photos from past holidays bring back happy memories.

We know this and I bet all of you have similar anchors.

But where's this going to be useful when influencing people? Let me explain.

Firstly we have to do it subtly or in a covert manner. After all we don't want our customer to know what we're up to, do we?

Now think what kind of state of mind we want our customer to get into when we influence them. You might pick decisiveness. That would be jolly useful since they're more than likely be in a position to make a quick decision to our advantage.

So pace them carefully, match their physiology and other aspects you choose. Once you have the rapport, get them into the state you want. For decisiveness you might want to ask them to go back to a time when they made a really good decision. Explore it with them, probe more, listen intently and when you think they're immersed in the state of mind, create the anchor or memory jogger.

You might choose something visual or auditory. A facial expression on your part, a gesture maybe or a distinctive tone in your voice. Or both. I often use a touch at this point, subtly touching their shoulder. Or sometimes I'll raise my right hand and twist it slowly in front of them.

For me, when I'm on the training stage I create a timeline along the stage, from my right to my left. Seen by the audience I have a timeline which starts on their left and continues along the stage to their right. Most people have times or diaries which go from left to right. I create this by running through the agenda with them at the beginning, starting on their left and moving slowly across the stage until I hit their right. I then move to the position when I'm talking about something that happened in the past. You guessed it, I'm standing on their left hand side of the stage, where the time came from.

Subtly I've anchored the stage for them. The left hand side is the past and their right hand side is the future.

Once you've created this anchor you fire it off when you want them to have the state of mind.

When I'm presenting my proposal I'll subtly touch them on their shoulder or raise my right hand and slowly twist it. And when I'm presenting my proposal and mentioning the competition, I'll casually walk over to the "past" - their left hand side of the stage. And the past is well, passed.

And when I mention my idea, yep…I walk over to their right – their future anchored state.

Spatial Anchoring

Use your body and movement to help the sales process move along nicely.

That's right, your body and movement can help move things along. Anchoring is a term meaning to remind someone of a thought, an emotion by repeating a word or a gesture.

Mention a certain word and your memory floods back to relive the moment the word was created.

We live in rural Gloucestershire and one of the great things about that are the long walks available to us just on our doorstep. We always take Brodie, our Italian Spinone, a large breed gundog who relishes long walks, off the lead so she can dive into bushes and hedgerows searching for game birds. She loves to frighten them into the sky for the fictitious guns to shoot.

My favourite walk is a two hour affair which takes you to the peak of Sandhurst Hill with the wondrous views, down the other side, past the Red Lion pub along the banks of the River Severn which serves a luscious pint of Old Rosy, and then back along the meadows to home.

But the rest of the family hate the walk. The walk is called the Sandhurst Hill walk and every time I suggest we go for a walk I always say Sandhurst Hill to the tumultuous noise of "Oh no, not Sandhurst Hill, no way Dad".

Sandhurst Hill has become synonymous with long, arduous, exhausting trudge. The name has been anchored. In the same way with hypnotic sales we can anchor certain words but better still, body movement and gestures, to ensure the customer has a thought we want them to have. Here are some spatial anchoring ideas.

Backs to the wall

In heavy interruption areas such as coffee shops, hotel lobbies, reception areas, try and put yourself with your back to a wall or blank area so your client doesn't get distracted whilst watching you.

You can then use all sorts of gestures and non-verbal language to get your points across. You might get distracted but you can handle that can't you?

Move backwards

When you first meet a customer in person move backwards about a foot as soon as you make eye contact. This is a great little technique to show that you are non-threatening and do not want to put them under any undue pressure.

It gets the meeting off to a relaxed and level beginning. Try it next time you meet a customer, particularly in a retail environment where customers expect pushy salespeople…it works.

Sway your body

Use your body position. For example when you talk about your competition, move your body one way and for information about you and your service, move your body into a different position. Your client will anchor the information to the body position.

Use your hands

Hands? What do we do with them? When sitting down with clients, try to keep your hands below your face and above the table. This is the triangle zone. Keep them in this zone and use gestures but small ones. Hands to face does you no favours at all so keep them away from this area unless you want to do a classic thinking person's pose.

Standing to present, keep your hands in the zone between your belly button and chin – never below or above these places. Use them to gesture and describe, don't grasp them like there's no tomorrow.

Now start to use your hands and arms to anchor things.

"On one hand we could look at this option and on the other hand we could go this way". Now emphasise or gesture the hand you would rather they take. This is quite hypnotic by the way.

The Cooperative Angle

Always sit at 90 degrees to your client as this is known as the cooperative position but remember what's behind you.

Touching

Researchers operating in an American shopping mall demonstrated that a touch on the customer's upper arm for about half a second had a miraculous result.

- 63% of those shoppers touched, shopped for more.
- 23% of those shoppers touched, spent more money.

So the tip here is to lightly touch your customer's upper arm just before you want them to take some action. Buy your product, refer you on to someone else in the organisation, or sign the contract.

Chances are it'll increase your closing rates and help you influence your customer more.

You Gotta be in the Right Mood

I drink coffee, others meditate, some relax and some play a tune. It doesn't really matter what you do, but you have to be in the mood to do anything, especially if you're an Inside Sales Specialist.

Record bosses in the 1960s recognised that their artists needed to be in the mood before they recorded their numbers in the studio. To ensure Carole King recorded Tapestry successfully, they positioned her so she could see the band playing to allow her to coordinate the music. Karen Carpenter preferred to sit behind the drums before she was coaxed out slowly to sing in front of the audience.

Everyone has to be in the mood. But what happens if you get out on the wrong side of the bed?

You have to choose your mood. Here's how to choose your mood:

- Decide what state of mind you need for the task in hand. For example it might be "energetic".
- Think back to a time when you were full of this state, e.g. energetic.
- Go back in your mind's eye to that moment and recall the crescendo of the feeling.
- Create a reminder by touching something or singing a tune, or smelling something, or saying something.
- Repeat the process.

Hey presto, you've created an anchor, as we call it in NLP. Next time you need this same state of mind, just fire off the anchor or the reminder you set in the first place.

I've loads of anchors. I listen to particular tunes. I've burnt a CD for the car and have a playlist on my phone which has various tunes to give me different states. For an energetic state, which I need when I do my big talks, I use David Bowie's Queen Bitch. This also fires a visual reminder of the set on the Old Grey Whistle Test when Bowie and Mick Ronson are giving it large.

And I often say to myself "Give it large Paul, they're 'aving it large", a phrase from Teddy Sheringham, when my team won the Champion's League in 1999 and had all the energy needed right into stoppage time.

If I want a state of pure happiness, I press my posterior fontanelle at the back of my head. Google it if you want to know where this is. That fires back a visual and kinaesthetic anchor of lying on Blackpool Sands in June 1992 when I'd just proposed to my wife. A perfectly happy time.

Or I drink coffee, which always gets me picked up, or is the actual ritual of drinking it an anchor?

6 Secret Signals of Physical Success

It was 8 in the morning. Dublin was sublime. The early morning mist was drifting over the River Liffey and there I was, sitting in a client meeting, waiting for the boss to arrive. In she walked, or should I say glided. An entrance which exuded confidence, humility, accomplishment. A glide across the room which was practised and fluent. She oozed success with every movement.

How do some people do this? What secret do they have to make that perfect first impression? Read on to discover the Seven Secrets of Physical Success.

Entering the Room

The first impression is vital, everyone knows that. So when entering a room for the first time, maybe with a customer sitting at a desk or a meeting room, make sure your movements give the right first impression. The keys to entering a room are to stand tall and then do slow and deliberate movements.

Movement

Stand tall, actors use the wall to adjust their posture and stance. Stand with your back to the wall and this gives you the perfect posture to use. Then make every movement slow and deliberate. Fast jerky movements just give the wrong impression of nervousness. Make every movement deliberate and with a purpose. This might sound odd, but just watch people doing the same thing and their nerves will get the better of them via unnecessary movement. You see your nerves come through your periphery limbs. Your legs and arms are where we show our nerves. Legs show nerves through pointless movement. Every movement must have a purpose.

Smile

The human smile is the most important rapport building skill known to mankind. We've smiled for thousands of years as a peace gesture. It evolves from our times as apes when the smile showed no fighting intent, almost a submissive gesture amongst primates. A smile also injects your body full of endorphins, the body's natural "feel good" drug.

Posture

Your posture says reams about the person you are. Are you slouched, angled? Are your feet and legs balanced or do you lean from one to the other, constantly moving and shuffling. This is an art not a science and you can choose to stand whichever way you wish, after all it's a free world. But if you want to create a great first impression, stand solid and balanced. Feet about the same width as your shoulders and slightly angled away from your body, but not like a penguin! Legs still but using the knees as natural hydraulics.

Keep the body looking tall and confident. Arms by the sides when not in use and gesturing with full arms when the words require. The mid line from your forehead to the floor should never be blocked. Keep it open and clear to give a natural welcoming image.

A final point about posture. Do you stand or sit? In a large group setting you must stand to give a confident and persuasive talk. With two or three people, sitting is appropriate. If you are very tall, try to keep your eye level the same as the customer, so you might want to sit down to balance the eye level with your customer. Never look down on customers!

It's now been proven that your body affects your state of mind. A confident and assured stance and posture will make you feel good. And this has a knock on effect on your performance.

Eye Contact

Give plenty of it, as much as your customer. Take care with locking onto a nose or one eye. Try to gaze in a triangle across your customer's face. Eye to eye to mouth, back to eye and son on. This gives a warm friendly eye contact. When you're talking you want to give eye contact pretty much all the time but when listening, this is your chance to look away every now and then. Looking away and upwards sends the signal that you are listening and thinking about what the customer is saying.

With a group of people your eye contact must be shared amongst everyone in a natural style. Give each person 2 or 3 seconds of eye contact. No more, no less and share this contact around the room in a natural sporadic manner. Aim to keep your eyes on the audience 95% of the time. Be careful with slides or visual aids that take your eye contact away from the audience. In fact, challenge yourself if you use slides with lots of words and boring old bullets. Go on, ask yourself the question and honestly answer it. Are they merely your speech notes?

Breath

Take your time, most speakers are faster than they should be. Remember time travels differently when you are public speaking and it appears to go slower for us, therefore we try and rush things. Nerves make us rush our speech. Slow down and take breaths and relax at every breath you take. Have confidence with your pauses. Drink water if you wish or have some form of anchor to remind yourself to slow down.

The Performance Hierarchy

Many salespeople ask me, "How can I ensure my performance is the same day in day out, Paul? Some days I'm on a roll and I wish I could bottle it. Some days I'm not and I need to be able to change it. Can you explain how?"

Let me show you the Performance Hierarchy, which will explain how you can bottle your performance and produce the same day in day out. These hierarchies have been published before, often called success cycles or success formulas. They all have similar ingredients, don't they. They have thoughts which equal feelings, actions, results.

That kind of thing.

But the Performance Hierarchy is the mother of all of them because it takes you further -- the missing jigsaw piece which determines your performance. It takes you deeper to understand what you need to change to improve your performance.

Behaviour

Right at the top of the hierarchy is your performance, your actions, your observable skills and it's this we want to control so we perform at our best every day. Sustainable performance is the goal. Obviously good skills and excellent performance leads to fabulous results. That's been known for ages.

So what alters your behaviour, your performance? Many people advocate more skills training, coaching, development.

Now I agree, but for those who already have the right performance -- the behaviours that bring results -- our aim is to help them duplicate this so they perform consistently at a high ability. No increase in skills training will make much difference.

No, we need to help them at a deeper level, if we're looking for consistency of performance.

Thinking

Beneath behaviour is what you think. Your self-talk, your inner dialogue. We saw how this can be recognised or spotted, but I haven't told you how you can change or control your inner dialogue apart from telling you that it is a skill you need to master.

Feelings

What you think is influenced by your feelings. It makes sense really since how you feel affects what you think. If I feel sad, then I will think sad thoughts, so the only way to change my thinking is to alter my feelings and that's not easy. Some people go day by day having no control over their feelings and thus, have no control over their inner dialogue. Scary, isn't it.

So a trainer gets some bad vibes from a group member who is challenging their material and expertise and the trainer starts to feel awkward and stressed. This affects her self-talk which knocks on her behaviour and she starts getting defensive and needy which further feeds the group member. Out of control.

But you can alter your feelings by initially understanding and noting how you feel. Many people have little grasp beyond six basic feelings, typically – anger, excitement, sadness, fatigue and hunger. If you get wise at recognising the exact feeling you are having, you can make some good decisions about the actions resulting from that feeling and you can try to change how you feel.

But there's another way. Are you ready for the real secret to how you can control your results?

Emotions and Physiology

We need to go further. Beneath your feelings is emotion. Your emotions are scary things which are influenced by your physiology and this is an area many people don't explore, don't understand, and so don't use.

Let me explain because you'll like this.

Your physiology, your bodily functions are constantly sending your brain signals, data, information, and energy which are turned into emotions by your brain. And the emotions ripple upwards through the hierarchy affecting your feelings, then your thoughts, then your performance.

These emotions are merely the signals, the energy being generated from your body. Energy in motion or e-motion. Take the trainer getting hassle from a group member. The physiology will react to the threat in an instant. The heart rate will rise, chaotic breathing will occur, a stomach churning feeling will happen, skin will redden, beads of sweat will appear and this variety of signals as data sent to the brain will cause emotion which will make her feel anxious and worried about what they are saying.

This in turn knocks on the self-dialogue, the thinking, which resonates to the behaviour. The trainer goes all negative in her body language, quickens her speech showing nervousness, can't think straight, moves backwards negatively, apologises for what she said, and tries to be liked.

Wow. At last we can now explain why this behaviour occurred. We now have the key to change everything. It's right down at the core level, the physiology of the human being.

And the best news of this entire article is that we can do things to affect our physiology. Controlled breathing will do this immediately to counter any negative emotions. Anchoring, which we mentioned earlier, gets you to repeat a great moment in your mind. The brain literally gets the body to repeat its reactions that occurred when the event first took place. The same signals, data and energy flow, which re-create the emotion, then the feeling, then the thought, then the behaviour. Easy.

We talked about changing the body's data and energy through exercise and diet; these all work and produce the right physiology -- just being aware of how the body reacts to events. Keep proper check at the core of the hierarchy and the rest will follow.

At last, the secret to the universe.

Mastering the Motivation Cycle

Life has its ups and downs and we need strategies to handle these so we can have positive and supporting thoughts and beliefs about ourselves.

Agreed? I'm sure you agree.

But life has its ups and downs.

Negative Thoughts

And to cap it all, recent research has shown that for every positive thought we have, most of us will have 14 negative thoughts to go along with it and if we're not careful, these negative thoughts can soon drown out that precious positive thought.

Every day we're being bombarded with negative media reports. Just take a look at the front page of today's BBC website:

Belgian passenger trains collide

Two Belgian commuter trains collide outside Brussels, with latest estimates of the death toll ranging from at least 10 to 25.

▶ Video from the crash scene
▶ 'People were scattered all over'
· In pictures: Belgium train crash

OTHER TOP STORIES

▸ UK soldier shot dead in Helmand
▸ Tory 'worker co-operatives' plan
▸ Couple in £56m EuroMillions win
▸ Sydney terror plotters sentenced
▸ Rape victims 'to blame' - survey
▸ Tory error over teen pregnancies
▸ Adverts tackle teen domestic violence

Taliban bombs 'slow Afghan push'

Improvised bombs placed by Taliban fighters are slowing Nato's big offensive in Afghanistan, military officials say.

Mobile firms unite to offer apps

Twenty-four of the largest phone operators join together to make it easier to sell and distribute mobile phone apps.

ALSO IN THE NEWS

Single recorded to help Haiti's earthquake victims tops chart

WINTER OLYMPICS 2010

Canada secure historic gold me‹

▸ German Loch wins luge gold medal
▸ As it happened - Winter Olympics day three

VIDEO AND AUDIO NEWS

Snow causes car pile-up in Kansas
▶ Watch

▶ Watch BBC News headlines

Abducted girl reunited with family
▶ Watch

◀ Listen Radio news summary

It's just a constant stream of bad news, which has a negative effect on our beliefs and attitude.

Let's have a look at how we can control them first before we go and end it all.

Understanding the motivation cycle can help us control our beliefs and thinking.

The Motivation Cycle

Feeding from the Performance Hierarchy, we add to the top the three circles.

A good result in sales or in our lives makes us feel good and we get positive thoughts and this embeds our beliefs. This gives us confidence.

This fuels the motivation to take more action. Taking more action will give us results and good results create positive thoughts and confidence. And so on and so on.

It's a never ending cycle and it's where we get the phrase "I'm on a roll" or "I'm on a downward spiral". Relying just on good results and good news is not practical as these don't happen all the time. It's like waiting for the phone to ring bringing you lots of new business – yes, it happens occasionally – but if you rely on that strategy to achieve your sales targets, then you're doomed.

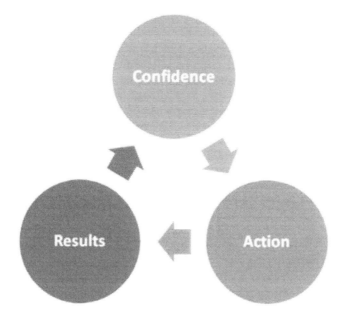

SMS – your Sales Motivation System

I help to run and coach our village Under 12s Junior Rugby Team called the Bredon Buzzards. Look us up on the web www.bredonbuzzards.com

At the beginning of this season, we got off to a great start -- winning our first two matches convincingly, but then the rot set in and we lost five matches on the bounce.

Now you can imagine that by Christmas, the boys were feeling pretty depressed and as for the coaching team, we were distraught... devastated.

We began to question our abilities and drive, our motivation dropped, we kept debating our coaching strategies, questioning ourselves, blaming ourselves... we panicked.

Does this ring a bell in sales or management when times get tough – maybe a lean spell, a period of bad news and unforced errors?

How do we rise above it? One way is my SMS or Sales Motivation System.

The secret to an SMS is to break down what you do and rather than wait until a major success like a big sale, you reward yourself for achieving the small increments that lead to the goal. And when you reward yourself regularly for the small achievements, you boost your motivation and self-esteem.

BREDON BUZZARDS
2007/2008 SEASON

Let me explain what we did at Bredon Buzzards. We sat down and examined our coaching system and training drills. We broke down what it was during a game that led to tries and points being scored and eventual victories.

We talked about winning scrums, line-outs, rucks, mauls, passing without dropping the ball, tackling well. We then devised new Skill Drills to practise these core elements and rewarded the boys when they did these things well -- especially during matches.

All the little rewards started to have an effect on our motivation and the kids' drive. Even if we lost a match, which we did early in the New Year, we still remunerated ourselves for winning scrums, tackles, line outs, etc... and soon enough we had our first, very narrow, victory and haven't looked back since.

So break down your sales process or your coaching process into smaller chunks and reward yourself with points or Mars bars, it doesn't matter. The fact that you achieved the small segments will eventually lead to a big success, a sale or a rugby victory.

The strange twist though, is what the boys really thought. Apparently they weren't too bothered about losing every match. By the time they had arrived home, been dipped into a bath and fed a roast dinner, washed down with copious amounts of ginger beer... they had totally forgotten the game, preferring to remember the fun they had with their mates.

It was us parents and coaches who took it all to heart and worried about things. Dwelled on and resented the referee's decisions. Perhaps we should learn to think more like a 12 year old and not grow up so quickly.

Marketing Points System

Many of you might use the water cooler at work to do it, some people use Facebook for it, others Link In.

I go to coffee mornings to do it. I'm talking of membership of various associations which helps me keep abreast of the latest issues and developments in my profession and network. And naturally what's involved with association membership? Attending meetings.

My wife jokes and calls them my coffee mornings.

But a day's attendance at an association meeting is worth 25 points to me and it's well worth it.

Leaving a mobile phone message with a client is worth 5 points, if I get through and have a brief conversation, that's worth 10 points. Writing this article is worth 10 points, making it into a podcast and uploading to iTunes is worth 15 points, speaking to an industry event pro bono gives me 50 points. Getting a testimonial to put on my website carries 3 points; a new client meeting culminating in a proposal weighs in at a portly 75 points.

And my weekly marketing and prospecting target is 100 points, so I make doubly sure I achieve it every week as one of my sales metrics.

Think about your sales role. Do you prospect and market continually, a little every day? Can the points system work for you? Try writing down all the methods that you employ to market your business and just like everything in life, variety is the spice.

You might have:

- Running Seminars
- Mailings
- Newspapers ads
- Email publications
- Networking – breakfast clubs etc.
- Articles in trade magazines
- Referrals
- Twitter, LinkedIn, Facebook etc.
- Testimonials
- Cold Calling

Now make a note of how effective they are and how much effort is required and then give each one a points score. Finally decide how many points you need to achieve each week and make this a personal metric or target to achieve.

It makes you do it, it ensures you have a variety of methods of prospecting, it lets you do a little every day and you get to reward yourself at the end of the week when you've done it.

One of my favourite pieces of marketing is association meetings, also known as coffee mornings to my wife. But the homemade blueberry cake I had last Friday was to die for; well worth 25 points.

How to Boost Your Self-Motivation

Here in the UK we've been enjoying dollops of the white stuff – snow. It's amazing what snow can do to the landscape.

For anyone who has had building work done, you know what the aftermath looks like. Ours is no different – outside of the new conference room, it looks like the Somme battlefield on steroids. Builder's rubble in every nook and cranny, old bricks, cement, plasterboard, tangled metal. A sight for sore eyes it is.

But following a 2 hour blizzard, the mess had all disappeared. The field looks brand new as though construction had never happened. It looks beautiful with the white snow glistening in the sunshine.

And it struck me then that in life, we all have set-backs which beat us backwards and these issues can affect us all. Some dwell on them – some move on. We need a way to cover them up and move on otherwise our self-motivation will take a battering. We could do with snow to cover them up for us.

Whether we're in sales or sales coaching, we have to be self-motivated to succeed in what we do. Yes, we can be motivated externally with targets, rewards, success and recognition but these don't happen continuously, so we have to have inner self motivation to pull off our goals.

We all have knock-backs, we all make mistakes. The trick is to learn from them. Extract what you learnt so you don't repeat it, jot it down somewhere. I have a pocket diary where I jot down all my learnings and ideas when they crop up. If I make a mistake, I note down what I learnt from it and then try to wipe out the memory so I can move forward.

Now that's the hard part.

So when we make a mistake, remove what you learnt, note it down, cover up the mistake with a snow blizzard, pick yourself up and move on. Don't let previous mistakes bug you as this serves no value. That way your self-motivation will carry on unhindered.

And if you do drift back to the mistake, imagine a beautiful white snow blizzard rolling in from the east which will cover up any blemishes on the landscape within minutes.

But be quick, as snow will melt to reveal the builder's rubble once again. Looking outside now that the snow's gone reminds me to order a skip, and spend a weekend getting rid of the rubbish permanently. And with the warm weather on us, I bet Claire is just waiting to ask me too. Can't wait.

Acting "As If"

NLP or Neuro Linguistic Programming gives us acting "as if" which is a really neat technique to help us perform better at our jobs as salespeople.

Let me explain.

Acting "as if" enables you to mimic whatever you're trying to do and to act "as if" you're already doing it. For example I made a client visit at the end of last year to a real tough cookie. His PA mentioned he was an impatient, alpha male, type A personality. Now that's not me but all I did was to act "as if" I was, so I matched his style during the meeting.

So next time you need:

- More self confidence
- A calm state of mind
- More patience

- The ability to speak well in public
- To close more effectively in a sales meeting

Just act "as if" you were doing these things and trick your mind into believing that you can really do it. Say to yourself; I'm going to act "as if…"

Thank NLP for this technique and yes, you can get jabs for this at the chemists.

The Edison Success Formula

Have you ever had to tackle something that you haven't the faintest idea how to achieve it? What a daunting prospect, but Thomas Edison was famous for inventing things which he really didn't have an idea how to create.

Edison taught us all how to cope with set- backs and fiercely persevere until you reach success. Let me explain the Edison Success Formula as this might help you to deal with set-backs and defeats in your working life and how to use change to your advantage.

The Edison Strategy looks like this:

Describing the Edison Cycle

We start with a clear purpose – a goal and direction. We then sit down to work out a plan of action and then we take action on our plan.

Now ideally the action you take brings results. If it doesn't, invite feedback.

Good salespeople will self-analyse every sales meeting and give themselves feedback. You might be able to get feedback from others. Handling feedback is a major skill.

How to Handle Feedback

Here's how:

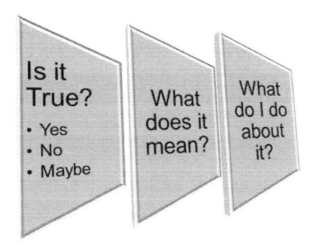

Accept the feedback and ask yourself; is it true? Do you rate the person who gave it to you, can you trust the integrity of their feedback, have others said similar things? Is it true?

Yes or no or maybe.

If it's true, find out what it means and what should you do about it. Take action and work out how you'll change…then forget about it.

By the way, if the feedback wasn't true, then forget about it immediately. And don't dwell on it.

A friend of mine relies heavily of audience feedback for his speeches. If he gets a negative piece of feedback he often dwells of this forever. And that's even if he gets one negative amongst a pile of 200 responses!

Make the change, re-evaluate your plan and take action again. Edison did this a reputed 10,000 times before he created the first light bulb. Hopefully you'll not need this many attempts at reaching your success.

Mastering your Communication with NLP

What has flying in an aeroplane to Iran got to do with overcoming the famous objection "that's too expensive"? A lot, in fact, so let me begin.

Before you start reading this chapter, I'd like you to do something for me. Next to the statements that appear below, please write down your first reaction. It doesn't matter what that is, but it must be your initial thought. We'll come back to this later in the chapter.

- Red hair
- Bulldog jaw
- Close set eyes
- Feeble handshake
- Can't look you in the eye

Let's start with the basics of traditional communication. I'm no Luddite, but I want to get away from mobile phones, email, webcams and the like and focus my attention on face-to-face selling.

The 3 Vs – Visual, Verbal, Vocal

So what do we use when selling to people? We use the 3 Vs – visual methods, vocal usage and verbal words to make some sense. We all use these three methods in our face-to-face meetings and lots of research has tried to categorise which is most important. The consensus puts visual first, vocal second and verbal – the words themselves – way down the pecking order, which is actually very true.

Visual or body language in any culture dominates selling. People are influenced by first impressions and the way we look and behave visually. I like to quote the 90:90 rule – during the first 90 seconds of meeting someone face-to-face, you'll develop an impression that will stand the test of time, or at least 90% of that impression will last. In selling, this is so important. Get it right in the first couple of minutes and the rest may well be plain sailing. Get it wrong and you're on an upward struggle to regain the customer's confidence.

The vocal side shouldn't be underestimated either. Just by the way you say something will determine how your client accepts the words. People's voices bristle with tonality, pace and volume, which all contribute to a message. When I get home from my business trip, my wife will greet me at the front door and just by the way she says my name, I will know what kind of mood she is in. My wife is brilliant at knowing if I'm telling the truth, just by the way I say things. Scary.

The words themselves can be so misinterpreted. I recall a true story based in the 1950s in London. On a smoggy night two likely lads robbed a warehouse in the East End of London. Not particularly good at the robbing game, they were soon tailed by a policeman who followed them up to the top of a warehouse building and cornered them successfully. Derek Bentley was reported to have said to his accomplice, who had the gun, "Let him have it". I guess Chris, having watched too many westerns at the cinema, understood his good friend and promptly shot the policeman dead.

Later in the Crown Court, the prosecution successfully tried and hanged Derek for being the cause of the murder by influencing Chris to kill the policeman. The defence unsuccessfully tried to convince the jury that the words "let him have it" meant to give the gun to the policeman. Derek was hanged shortly afterwards. Chris survived because he was a juvenile.

Early this century, Derek's relatives successfully had him posthumously pardoned, so maybe sense prevailed.

So, for salespeople like ourselves, we must remember that selling is not just about words, benefits, features and the like, but the way we say them, the way we look and act and how we deliver the words. Also, the way we smile and build a rapport and the way we gain trust in the first 90 seconds. And this is a major cornerstone of what Rapport Selling is all about.

We know that to sell to someone we must use all three methods – visual, vocal and verbal – but the million dollar question is, what stops our message from getting through?

The NLP Communication Barriers

The answer is that humans have developed communication filters that dominate our thinking. If we, as salespeople, fail to respect this and use it to our advantage, we'll not become precision Rapport Sellers.

Let's go back to the little bit of work I asked you to do at the beginning of this article. What did you put down for red hair? Was it fiery, excitable, short tempered? What about someone who can't look you in the eye? Was it sheepish, untrustworthy, or some other negative reaction?

It doesn't matter – the point is that all of us, including myself, have pre-conceptions that taint our opinions of these characteristics. These pre-conceptions evolve from our years of experiences, memories, beliefs, judgements, teachings and so dominate our everyday beliefs. As salespeople we need to know and understand these so we can adapt our selling to get through them.

NLP revealed three filters – deletions, distortions and generalisations. A knowledge of these helps salespeople understand people more intimately than before and enables us to tighten up our sales techniques.

Deletions

Deletions happen all around us. Purely to make sense of the world around us, we have to delete information. Right now I'm in an aeroplane taking off from London Heathrow airport and I'm being bombarded with signals and information. If I tried to focus on everything around me, my brain would probably explode. No, to make sense of everything I'm only able to concentrate on about 7 signals, the rest are either ignored or put over to my autopilot. I can sense the laptop, my ears popping, my ideas in my brain, the smell of the in-flight food being prepared, how uncomfortable I feel in my cramped seat. Everything else, the worry about the flight, the turbulence, my bodily functions and so on are all being ignored or placed into autopilot.

NLP calls your autopilot your subconscious. That's OK, but it does conjure up images of hypnotists and the like and some people have a negative reaction to that.

Much of our world is on autopilot. Driving a car is virtually all autopilot - I mean the actual controls of the car – the gears, the clutch, the brakes, the steering. This leaves the road ahead and our decision making ability totally at the front of our minds. This is one of the reasons why mobile phones are so dangerous when driving, since much of our attention is focused on the conversation. Whether we hold the phone or not, the focus on the conversation is dangerous. Remember, we only have the ability to work with about 7 signals.

In selling, ignore deletions at your peril. When meeting your customer, beware of all the distractions that might take up one of these 7 allowable signals. If there are too many, then you might be deleted. Perish the thought. Don't overload the customer with too much information as you can quickly fill up their 7 signals. In selling, the phrase "less is more" really counts, so make sure you understand their needs and only give them benefits that mean something to them.

Asking For Referrals

Here's a neat tip I learnt in Iran. The next time you want to ask your customer for referrals at the end of the sales meeting, try making your request for your client's assistance whilst you fiddle with your watch. Remove your watch from your wrist, fiddle with it and put it back on your wrist. I hear you asking, "Why?" Do it and note your customer's reaction. They will focus on your watch and your words of request will go straight into their subconscious and will be automatically translated into their own words. They will oblige -- you wait. In a way, you are hypnotising them into giving you names of their friends who might need your help. This is the basis of hypnotic suggestions used by stage hypnotists. It really works, try it.

Without deletions, there would be no ability for you to use other hypnotic selling techniques. Now you wouldn't want this to escape, would you? We've got some great articles on this subject, just contact me.

Buckaroo and Attention Spans

I remember fondly on wet Sunday afternoons playing Buckaroo. You loaded up this spring mounted plastic horse with all sorts of plastic items – spades, boxes, blankets – the items got heavier and heavier and eventually the horse would bolt out of the springs, scaring you witless.

Great fun.

You see there was only so many things the horse could carry before it bolted and that's a little like humans and their attention spans.

NLP says that we can only concentrate on around 7 things. Only keep around 7 items in our head, in our conscious mind. Beyond that and we bolt like buckaroo.

We obviously don't bolt but if we are faced with handling more than 7 things, we ignore them or our subconscious takes care of them. And that's where we can influence effectively. Let me explain some uses:

Make sure when you're dealing with a customer or colleague that you want to influence, keep the distractions to a minimum. Apart from the obvious, be aware of what's behind you, it's amazing what can distract. Remember 7.

Deliberately overload the customer and then slip in some hypnotic influencing techniques. Here's a couple of them:

- Use the word "because" liberally to justify your reasons for your idea
- Soften your voice and lower it for an influential tone
- Match everything you can see and hear about your customer

There's a whole list of things you can do whilst the customer is occupied and these serve to influence them. Its ok, it's only influencing.

Distortions

The second filter that prevents our sales messages from getting through are distortions. These are dangerous because we distort the real meaning of a message to be totally what it wasn't intended to be. Right now, I'm travelling to Tehran to help run a two-day sales conference. Now people distort the real intentions of the Iranian people because of TV information and other media.

We see demonstrations from mobs outside the British and American embassy on the TV and we see their President giving rhetoric to the world's media. From this carefully selected news we distort the real meaning. Deep down the Iranians or Persians, as many prefer, are a peaceful nation dedicated to their religion with a love of family life and togetherness. Extremely friendly and hospitable, young and excitable, the nation of Iran has so much to offer the world. The world's media has only distorted our understanding.

We have to be careful with our customer's ability to distort information we give them. Make it clear and precise and help them to relate the features into worthwhile benefits.

Generalisations

The last and most useful filter for us to understand is generalisations. The world is full of these. When I asked you to note what your thoughts were with the red hair, close set eyes, you gave me generalisations which have grown within you due to your experiences, values and beliefs.

You can't stop people making generalisations, that's life. People do it to help them understand the enormous amount of data thrust upon them every day of their lives. Generalising just helps us tick over and move on.

But for the Rapport Seller, appreciating how people will generalise helps us to move the sale along. Knowing that people generalise helps us to probe deeper to find out their real needs. When we ask initial questions, we get replies but these are often just generalisations that we need to probe and dig deeper to get beyond the surface of the subject. "What's important to you in the car you buy?" might get a fairly scant first reply – "Economy and a comfortable ride." "What makes you say that?" is a great question to ask since it drills below the generalisation, and we might get a more thoughtful answer.

"What are you looking for in your mortgage?" will probably give you something around "cheap" and this should be followed up with probes such as, "Do tell me, what does cheap mean to you?" or "I'm curious to know, what do you mean by cheap".

Objection handling is made easier when we appreciate these generalisations. Sometimes if we've not tested the temperature beforehand and closed our customer too early, we get objections. Now often these are generalisations such as "I'll think about it", or "It's too expensive". A customer's first reactions when forced is to throw up a generalisation about our product, a first defence mechanism to give them time or to throw us off the scent. Probe on these.

Knee Jerk Reactions

As a small child, I was fascinated when doctors would carefully tap a patient's knee with a small hammer and the patient's leg would involuntary kick upwards. That's where the phrase "knee jerk reaction" comes from. For years after first seeing this on TV, I tried in vain to make my knee do the same with plenty of bruises to show for my efforts.

Life is full of knee jerk reactions. People get used to reacting in a certain way, especially when they are being offered to buy something. You see, when faced with a decision to buy something, we will revert to a knee jerk reaction and say something like, "No thanks" or "I'll think about it" or "Send/email me some brochures".

Unfortunately, many salespeople or those on the front line who need to sell things, accept these customer reactions and don't close on the sale. And this is a shame because often, knee jerk reactions are not real reasons.

The secret is to accept them for what they are... knee jerk reactions and kind of ignore them and try again. Throw in a holding phrase and re-do your close. If done carefully and subtly, it won't harm and may get the customer to think it through again and make a positive decision.

Some favourite responses that won't offend:

"That's fine, I'm only asking for a short chat with our adviser, it won't harm, will it?"

"I understand, however the benefits are excellent…."

"Are you sure? You'll be missing out on… "

"I could email you some brochures, but I've a better idea -- let's meet shortly to talk it through… "

Bear in mind, a customer's first reaction to your close, is normally a "no" because this is an inbuilt knee jerk reaction.

Our Own Knee Jerk Reactions

The second, more significant knee jerk reaction comes from us, the salesperson. When a customer gives us an objection or reservation which might be entirely understandable and realistic, we immediately come in with a pre-thought answer to the objection. Especially if we've just come back from a training course and we know all the answers to common objections.

Again the trick is to react differently. A nifty little reminder here is to imagine sitting on their lap. Of course, this is a metaphor and not something to actually do, although that depends on your customer I guess. No, I'm saying we follow the LAP rule – L for listen to the reservation and really hear them out first, then we A acknowledge it. I'm not saying agree with them but see their point of view, understand where they're coming from. And the final P is to probe to figure out exactly what it is they have an issue with.

"I can see where you're coming from there and it's a fine point you're making... can I just ask…... is that the only issue that might prevent you going ahead with this plan?"

This strategy gives you thinking time, ensures your customer knows they're being listened to and shows you're on their side.

So consider the two knee jerk reactions the next time you're in a sales situation. The customer's reaction to your close and your potential quick response to their reservation. Both hazardous in their own right.

And try as I may, I still can't get my knee to kick upwards every time I whack it with a hammer. Maybe if I hit it harder...

Tailoring Your Communication

What's The Point In Tailoring My Communication?

Because selling, when you strip it down to the bare bones, is communication. An effective salesperson is a master communicator, and one of the best techniques I can bring to you is the communication aspects from NLP – neuro linguistic programming.

I first learnt these in 1998, and now as a master practitioner I utilise NLP ideas throughout my training for salespeople. I just don't openly tell them it's NLP. The sales profession can be rather cynical.

This chapter will let you into the secrets of thinking styles so you can talk like your salesperson and understand how they like to communicate and hear/see/feel messages. And the eyes have it for when you want to know your salesperson's favourite style.

Let's start with your preferred thinking style, as I call it. It's the way you represent information in your head and how you like to both give and receive communication. This questionnaire will give you an early insight, and then I'll explain it all and how it can be useful when selling.

On the next page is a questionnaire which will give you an indication of your preferred style. Let's start here then I'll explain how you can use this..

NLP Thinking Styles Questionnaire

4	=	Closest to describing you
3	=	Next best description
2	=	Next best
1	=	Least descriptive of you

I am more likely to say:

☐ Important decisions are matters of feeling

☐ Important decisions are ones I tune in to

☐ Important decisions show my point of view

☐ Important decisions are logical and thoughtful

I am someone:

☐ With a nicely modulated voice

☐ Who looks good

☐ Who says sensible things

☐ Who leaves people with a good feeling

If I want to know how someone is:

☐ I observe their appearance

☐ I check how they are feeling

☐ I listen to their tone of voice

☐ I attend to what they are saying

It is easy for me to:

☐ Modulate the volume and tuning on a stereo system

☐ Consider the most intellectually relevant points concerning an interesting subject

☐ Choose superbly comfortable furniture

☐ Find rich colour combinations

I believe that:

☐ I am very effective at making sense of new facts

☐ My ear is very attuned to the sounds in my surroundings

☐ I feel very sensitive to the clothing that touches my body

☐ I picture bright colours when I look at the room

If people want to know how I am:

☐ They should know about my feelings

☐ They should look at what I am wearing

☐ They should listen to what I say

☐ They should hear the intonations in my voice

I am more likely to:

☐ Hear what facts you know

☐ See the pictures you paint

☐ Get in touch with your feelings

☐ Tune in to your harmonious messages

I believe that:

☐ Seeing something makes it believable

☐ Hearing the facts about something makes it believable

☐ Feeling something makes it real and believable to me

☐ Hearing how something is said makes it believable or not

I feel that:

☐ I usually have a strong sense about the well-being of my family

☐ I can picture the faces, clothes and small visible details of my family

☐ I know the way my family thinks about most issues, especially their significant ideas about things

☐ I hear the intonation and inflections in any of the voices among my immediate family and can identify who it is instantly

When it comes to learning:

☐ I learn concepts

☐ I learn to do things

☐ I learn to hear new things

☐ I learn to see new possibilities

When I think about decisions I will probably:

☐ Decide that important decisions are a matter of feeling

☐ Decide that important decisions are the ones I tune in to

☐ Decide that important decisions are the ones I see clearest

☐ Decide that important decisions are logical and thoughtful

I can easily say that:

☐ Remembering how a friend sounds tunes me in

☐ Remembering what a friend looks like is a clear memory for me

☐ Remembering the things a friend says to me is a good idea

☐ Remembering how I feel about a friend is easy

Thinking Style Scoring

Copy your answers from the test to the lines below:

1		2		3		4		5		6	
K		A		V		A		D		K	
A		V		K		D		A		V	
V		D		A		K		K		D	
D		K		D		V		V		A	

7		8		9		10		11		12	
D		V		K		D		K		A	
V		D		V		K		A		V	
K		K		D		A		V		D	
A		A		A		V		D		K	

Next fill in the numbers associated with each letter. There will be five entries for each letter.

Question	V	K	A	D
1				
2				
3				
4				
5				
6				
7				
8				
9				
10				
11				
12				
Totals				
	Visual	Kino	Auditory	Digital

The 4 Main Thinking Styles

Visual people

People who are primarily visual tend to see the world in pictures. They achieve their greatest sense of power by tapping into the visual part of their brain.

Because they're trying to keep up with the pictures in their brains, visual people tend to speak quickly. They don't care how they get it out - they're trying to put words to the pictures in their minds. They talk about how things look to them, what patterns are emerging or whether things look bright or dark.

Auditory people

People who are more auditory tend to be more selective about the words they use. They have more resonant voices and their speech is slower, more rhythmic and more measured. Since words mean so much to them, they are careful about what they say. They tend to say things like "That sounds good to me" or "I can hear what you're saying".

Feeling or Kinaesthetic people

People who are more kinaesthetic tend to be even slower. They react primarily to feelings. Their voices tend to be deep, and their words are often spoken in a deliberate pace. They're always seeking something concrete. Things are "heavy" or "intense". They use words like "I'm trying to get in touch with this" or "I'm reaching for an answer".

Auditory Digital

This person will spend a fair amount of time talking to themselves. They will want to know if something makes sense. They will spend time working things out inside their heads and will tend to value process, system, structure and order. Everyone has elements of all four styles, but most people have one that dominates.

Recognising the Thinking Styles

Visuals

- Stand or sit with their head and/or body erect, with their eyes up.
- They will be breathing from the top of their lungs and their upper shoulders and breathe fairly rapidly.
- They often sit forward in their chair and tend to be organised, neat, well-groomed and orderly. Appearance is important to them.
- They memorise by seeing pictures, and are less distracted by noise.
- They often have trouble remembering verbal instructions because their minds tend to wander.
- Fast talkers.
- 'A picture is worth a thousand words'.
- Use picture descriptions during conversation.
- Interested in how things look.
- Must see things to understand them.
- Like visually based feedback.
- Use gestures that may be high and quick.

Auditories

- Will move their eyes sideways.
- They breathe from the middle of their chest.
- They typically talk to themselves and some even move their lips when they talk to themselves.
- They are easily distracted by noise.

- They can repeat things back to you easily.
- They learn by listening.
- Usually like music and talking on the phone.
- They memorise by steps, procedures, and sequences (sequentially).
- The auditory person likes to be TOLD how they're doing.
- Responds to a certain tone of voice or set of words.
- They will be interested in what you have to say about your programme.
- Medium to fast talkers.
- Translate conversation to sounds associated with topic.
- Excellent at repeating back instructions.

Kinaesthetic

- They breathe from the bottom of their lungs, so you'll see their stomach go in and out when they breathe.
- They often move and talk very slowly.
- They respond to physical rewards and touching.
- They also stand closer to people than a visual person does.
- They memorise by doing or walking through something.
- They will be interested in your proposal if it "feels right".
- They check out their feelings prior to expressing their thoughts.
- Very physical people and like to touch during conversation.
- They like to walk through something before doing it.
- Use gestures that are low and smooth.

Auditory Digital

- Spend a fair amount of time talking to themselves.
- They will want to know if your programme "makes sense".
- The auditory digital person can exhibit characteristics of the other major representational systems.
- Speak in a clipped, crisp monotone.
- Breathing patterns like an auditory, higher up in the chest.
- Dissociated from feelings.

Recognition Summary

Pattern	Visual	Kinaesthetic	Auditory	Auditory Digital
Language	Seems, look, bright, perspective focus and colourful	Feel, grasp, touch, firm, warm, cool, get a handle on	Tone, loud, rings a bell, sounds like, harmonious	Statistically speaking, reasonable, logical, know
Posture	Straight, erect, head and shoulders up	Curved, bowed, head and shoulders down	"Telephone" posture, head tilted to side	Arms folded, erect, head up
Body "type" and movements	Either thin or obese; tight, jerky	Soft, full, rounded; loose, flowing	Inconsistent body; between tight and loose	Soft, full; rigid
Breathing	High in chest	Low into abdomen	Full range	Restricted
Voice tonality, speed and volume	High, clear, fast and loud	Low, airy, slow and soft	Melodic, rhythmic variable	Monotone, clipped, consistent
Eye elevation in relation to others	Above others	Below others	Level often diverted down to listen	"Gazes" over others' heads

Selling to Visuals

To sell successfully to visual people requires using visual words in your sales presentation, inviting the prospect to use his or her mind's eye. For example:

"Imagine how these plants will look a year from now."

"Can you see the expression on your wife's face when you give her this ring?"

"Picture the increased productivity you will have with this new computer system."

Make liberal use of brochures, photographs, visual aids and, where appropriate, web based movies, films and DVDs. They fix the customer's attention, so that it is much harder for him or her to daydream about things unrelated to the product or service. Since you are using the prospect's natural language, he or she gets a clear understanding of your product or service and relates to you easily.

The Joys of Peripheral Vision

I'll always remember my mother for one thing. Her third eye at the back of her head. She could see what was going on around her and had terrific peripheral vision and as a mother bringing up three boys, this is an essential attribute.

Having peripheral vision is an extremely useful skill to master if your job is to deal with people and over the years, I've come across some real practical uses for this talent. Let me explain.

If you need to do presentations in your business, using peripheral vision has two huge advantages. Firstly it allows you to be aware of the audience en masse. You can gauge reactions of people along the left side of the room whilst you're maintaining eye contact with the people on the right. Peripheral vision will encourage you to give eye contact to everyone, which you simply have to do, to engage an audience.

Secondly, intensifying your peripheral vision before you start your presentation can actually reduce your nerves. This is a little known trade secret but intensifying our peripherals can literally trick the brain to stop being nervous. Cool.

In a sales situation, it can also be useful. When addressing a group of people in a business to business situation, you can keep an eye on the key decision makers whilst addressing the other people in the unit, thus ensuring everyone is with you.

If you're selling in retail to a couple, say husband and wife, address the wife but use your peripheral to ensure you engage with the husband as well. Peripheral is useful to maintain eye contact but keep an eye on distinguishable body language as well.

In customer care, when you're operating a till or queue of customers, you can use your peripheral vision to keep an eye on the queue of people waiting and their impatient reaction. That way you can use the reassuring comment __"I'll be with you very shortly"__. There's nothing worse than being totally ignored by the customer care person who is too intent on the person they're dealing with. Of course they should concentrate on them, but a quick smile or acknowledgement can go a long way in reassuring that you'll be dealt with soon.

Convinced? I'm sure you are but how can you exercise your peripheral vision muscle? Easily. Every now and then, when you have a spare moment, fix your view on a spot somewhere in the distance, blur your eyes and focus on your sideways vision. Try and stretch a little more every time and after a while you'll become a natural. Practice does make perfect.

One day technology might help us out. Whilst searching the web for reading glasses, I stumbled across a brand new invention. Tiny mirrors built into the frame so you can see behind you. I also read how police at the 2012 London Olympics had face recognition cameras built into their sunglasses, to spot suspected terrorists. Wow. However, nothing can replace my mother's legendary third eye.

Go Peripheral the Next Time You Get Nervous

In sales we're often called upon to negotiate deals or supplies and sometimes we need to get a little tough, but we don't want to damage our relationship. Here's a great tip on how you can do this.

I met a really interesting guy to talk to; the head of the IT Conference that I was speaking in on my second day in Iran. He was my age and we had so much in common – children of the same ages, similar hobbies – a really nice guy.

But suddenly I looked around and realised I was on in 5 minutes. About to face 750 people in a huge auditorium, I was 5 minutes away from walking up onto the stage.

And what happened? Adrenaline set in. It always does and any professional speaker will tell you that this is quite natural, so learn to deal with it. My adrenaline levels started to rise and I wasn't dealing with it. By the way I renamed nerves into adrenaline a while ago – it just sounds so much better. But they are the same thing.

So I thought – "Hold on Paul you need a tactic here to relax you before you go on stage." So I immediately thought of one that I teach all my delegates on my public speaking workshops.

Peripheral vision.

Apparently the brain cannot process having too much adrenaline and focussing on peripheral vision at the same time. So I quickly focused my attention on the speaker in front of me and worked my peripheral vision so I could see practically all around me.

And guess what? My adrenaline levels stated to decline, I relaxed and walked onto the stage.

It worked.

So next time you're faced with rather too much adrenaline than normal, try the peripheral vision technique – it seriously does work.

Help them visualise using it

Last night I was watching a programme on the TV which involved a young couple who had to make a big choice when it came to buying a new home.

One home was in the French Atlantic coastline, a beautiful stretch of land glistening in the warmth of the sunshine. The house was fantastic, 4 bedrooms, sun terrace and full of original features….

The other place was in Exmouth in Devon, equally sublime but didn't share the same climate. It was a two bedroom terraced Victorian house with a garden overlooked by plenty of others.

Two estate agents covered each region and you would have thought the French one would have won hands down because of the location and property. But no, the Exmouth agent just had a knack of presenting his property better.

He continually helped the couple to imagine what it would be like living there, what would they use the garden for, who they would invite to the barbeques, when would they nip down to the sea, where would they fit their furniture…and so on.

Once they'd had the tour of the property in Exmouth, they could see themselves living there.

Now the poor agent in France did none of this. She pointed out good features but just kept on talking and talking and talking. And then more talking.

You can guess which one they chose.

So think about how you present your product or solution and help your customer to own it. Help them to visualise how they would use it.

If you sell insurance, as many of our readers do, before you do any questioning strings, help them visualise what it's like to be in a wheelchair or to be too weak to climb the stairs, let alone get back to work to earn some money. Help them see this, smell it, experience it in their mind's eye.

If you sell real estate, help them see what it'll be like to live there, imagine their new lifestyle.

If you sell big TVs, help them imagine what it would be like to sit on the sofa watching England beat Brazil in the final.

Don't tell them, help them to visualise it. Use questions to steer their thinking and imagination.

England 2 – Brazil 1. Now that's something rather delicious to visualise.

Visual is Where It's at

Have you used Uber? It's the app for your phone that's taking over the world's city transportation. And if you're a cab driver, you'll be up in arms about their taking over your business.

But I'm not going to debate that issue, just how good their app is.

When you call a cab, you can see on a map, in real time, the arrival of your car. You see it graphically moving along the road until it reaches your destination. No need for words or descriptions, it's just pure visual.

How good is your visual?

How much visual do you provide in your coaching sessions? Do you create diagrams; use an iPad to show graphics and pictures, photos?

What about in selling? Perhaps you carry around a packet of whiteboard pens and you draw illustrations on the boardroom white board rather than boring people with a whirring PowerPoint.

And your PowerPoints? Yes they are mostly pictures, images and photos aren't they?

In your webinars and Skype sessions, do you take every opportunity to show a graphic rather than talking, maybe share your screen if that serves to visualise? Do you even have your video on the screen, that's visual.

In telephone seminars, you could ask the audience to join you on a padlet. Padlet.com is a useful app that allows your audience to interact on the screen whilst the seminar is running.

Everybody expects visual nowadays, Uber have shown this to the transportation industry which, sadly, is being left behind in their wake.

Selling to Auditories

Learn to speak the language of the sound-oriented customer. Do so by using the sound words. Suggest to customers that they tune in to what other people say about what they bought.

Spend time just talking with them. Slow down a tad, learn to savour each word.

Use audio clips on your website to attract them – they want to hear your voice.

When called for, give your sound-oriented customer the phone numbers of two or three satisfied customers. When he or she hears what these people say, it will have a positive impact.

When you speak the sound language used by your sound-oriented customers, they will feel you understand them. You will be in harmony.

Selling to Kinos

To sell successfully to the action/feeling customer, use movement, feeling and action-based words. Let the customer get a feel for your product or service and how it operates, handles, fits or drives.

Involve your action/feeling customers physically whenever possible. Have them walk through the office with you. Make them sit down and type something on the keyboard. Let them touch the brochures.

The action/feeling language works best with customers who have this kind of information preference. Clues have already been given about how these customers talk and look.

Persuading customers through touch

In NLP we have this concept called anchoring which, like Pavlov's Dogs, allows you to attach a signal to a feeling. Pavlov rang a bell and made his dogs salivate.

But a lot of people know that story.

Natural anchors are sprinkled throughout your life. A special perfume aroma brings back a memory, smells work well and my favourite is gasoline which reminds me of cutting grass when I was 16 for some very rich people who owned a mansion and had au pairs sunbathing in the garden. Now that memory makes me feel good.

Sounds do the same, a tune reminds you of a holiday, an event. The Olympic logo helps people have positive feelings about GB and the country we live in.

I help salespeople create anchors to relive experiences where they had a particularly good state of mind which they would like again. These are often physical anchors such as a touch of the ear lobe or pressing a knuckle or pushing the oyster on the back of the head. If you don't know where that is, ask a sniper.

Sorry about that pattern interrupt, caught you though.

Today I'd like to share with you how you can use anchors with a customer that's so subtle yet impressively powerful.

Let me explain.

Touch is an incredibly powerful signal and touching people creates an electric current that literally zips through people. So here's the drill.

When you meet someone, a customer, a coachee, a stranger and you want to know their name, ask them and at the same time, smile broadly with locked-on eye contact and lean across and touch them between the elbow and shoulder of their right arm. This touch has now begun to be anchored and there's a connection between the two of you. The anchor you've created has good resonance, their name, you, big smile, eye contact – good feelings.

Now use this touch again when you want to recreate that good experience and positive state. Perhaps when you've presented your solution or idea you could lean across, touch their arm and say "Can you feel how good this could be for you?"

Or you might want them to make a decision, lean across and touch their anchored point and say "Take your time with this important decision, it does feel right though, don't you think?"

Rather hypnotic and dead cool. It does work, try it.

Selling to Auditory Digitals

They love lists. If you share an idea with them, give them time to 'discuss' it with themselves before requiring a response. They will rarely be spontaneous as they will want to 'think things through'.

Give them more time generally. Use flowcharts, structures. Share an agenda of the meeting with them and let them know their progress.

Use logical language. For example "There are 3 main benefits of this kind of mortgage. Number one is... number two is... "

"Does that make sense?"

The Perfect Test Close

Whenever I get the opportunity to observe and coach salespeople in action, one of the most popular requests for help is closing. "I just don't seem to want to close my customers... I guess I'm afraid of the reaction they'll give me." And fair play, no one likes rejection.

How do I help them? I show them how to test close, which once explained, people pretty much say "I already do that." "How" I respond. "I ask them how they feel".

"All the time?" I'd challenge. "Yes, anything wrong with that?" they would say defensively.

"No but it's a bit repetitive, try tailoring it to the thinking style of the customer so it has greater meaning and resonates with them."

Check the eye movements.

If they generally move their eyes upwards, then they prefer to communicate in visual ways so use visual words.

"What benefits do you see there?"

"How does that appear to you?"

If they move their eyes sideways, they probably prefer more auditory communication. You know words and sounds, so…

"How does that sound to you?"

"Tell me your thoughts on that one?"

Finally if they move downwards with their eyes, down right, then they're probably more kinaesthetic or feelings based communicators, so ask them.

"How do you feel about that?"

"Tell me what are you thinking?"

Try it next time you want to close your customers more without them knowing that you're closing. That's clever stuff.

Using Similar Language to Your Clients

What do you notice about the following four sentences?

- You have shown me a bright idea on how to proceed and I would like to look into it further.
- You have told me of a way to proceed that sounds good and I would like to hear more about it.
- You have handed me a way to proceed that is on solid ground and I would like to get more of a feel for it.
- You have provided me with a way to proceed that makes sense and I would like have more details.

The first sentence uses visual words, the second auditory, the third kinaesthetic and the fourth uses words that are not sensory based (auditory digital), yet all four sentences convey the same general meaning.

Our preferred thinking style affects the language we use to describe what is happening for us. The following table gives a list of the most widely used words for each of the thinking styles.

Visual

see
look
bright
clear
picture
dawn
reveal
illuminate
imagine
sight for sore eyes
take a peek
tunnel vision
bird's eye view
naked eye
paint a picture

Auditory

hear
tell
sound
resonate
listen
silence
squeak
hush
tune in/out
rings a bell
quiet as a mouse
voiced an opinion
give me your ear
loud and clear
on another note

Kinaesthetic

grasp
feel
hard
scrape
touch
get hold of
tap into
pull some strings
sharp as a tack
smooth operator
throw out
firm foundation
get a handle on
get in touch with
hand in hand
hang in there

Auditory Digital

sense
experience
understand
change
insensitive
conceive
know
think
learn
process
decide
figure it out
make sense of
pay attention to
word for word
without a doubt

KAV Openings Rule OK

KAV, what's that? It's a rule for opening any presentation or training session that you're doing. We all know how important it is to get off to a great start, to engage the audience, to compel them to want to listen further.

Here's how.

KAV – kinaesthetic, auditory and visual – in that order.

Start off with something that has feeling, emotion, humour – that's the kinaesthetic or kino start. Use a story that explains who you are. I have a couple of favourites I use that really show who I am, have humour, emotion contained.

Maybe humour – something funny in the news might do – don't tell jokes. Something funny that happened to you on the way in. Emotion, sentiment, passion.

Then comes auditory; lower your voice, make it resonant, bring in vocal variety – people want to hear your voice next to really connect and then finally comes…

Visual, in a picture on screen or image painted in their minds.

KAV rules OK. Next time you're planning a presentation or training session, use the KAV start.

Building Rapport

The Power of Rapport

It could've ended in a disaster and an international debacle except for a little thing called rapport.

10 US Navy sailors were detained after one of their two vessels broke down during a training mission in the Gulf in late 2015. Those detained - nine men and one woman - were taken to Farsi Island, in the middle of the Gulf, where Iran has a naval base.

US Secretary of State John Kerry called Foreign Minister Javad Zarif shortly after the incident. The pair developed a personal rapport during the nuclear talks.

As a result, Iranian state media said the group was released into international waters after apologising. The incursion was "unintentional", a statement from the Revolutionary Guards quoted by state media said.

Now that's the power of rapport. Here's some tips to remind you how.

- Seek common ground

- Maintain eye contact and a respectful distance
- Smile copiously
- Compliment the other person genuinely
- Match their thinking styles – visual, auditory, kino
- Match energy levels
- Match physiology

Yawning and Rapport

We've known for ages that a yawn is contagious. Someone in the group yawns and someone will yawn in return, often instantaneously or within 5 minutes. The reason, we also know, is down to the desire to be alike, to be an equal, to create similarity.

Researchers in Italy's Pisa University found that the "yawn transmission" was quicker amongst those that already had rapport – close friends and lovers.

The study is based on a rigorous behavioural data collection carried out for over one year on more than 100 adults, corresponding to more than 400 "yawning couples". People have been observed in a wide array of natural contexts: during meals, on the train, at work, etc. Observations, carried out in Italy and Madagascar, have involved people of different nationalities, and with a different degree of familiarity: strangers and acquaintances (colleagues and friends of friends), friends, kin (parent/offspring, grandparent/grandchild, and siblings), and mates.

So it's been scientifically proved that people who like other people want to be the same and that building a rapport can be accelerated by matching and mirroring the person you want to build rapport with.

So next time you're in a situation where rapport will move the relationship further in the right direction, follow this 5 minute induction whilst engaging in your first conversation:

1. Shake hands with the person to calibrate their energy levels, and match the energy.
2. Matching energy will allow you to match their voice – tone and pace.
3. Calibrate their face first – smile, expressions and amount of eye contact – and match this.
4. Go peripheral in your vision to observe their overall physiology – body language – posture, position and match this.
5. If their posture changes, delay the match for about 20 seconds.
6. Now pick up their gestures they use when speaking, notice them carefully and match these, but only when you talk.

7.   When you have the rapport, you'll know inside. To test, you could alter your physiology a little and watch as they match you.

And if they yawn…don't match this, instead end the meeting because you're boring them.

Begin the Rapport Building Process

Rapport…does it mean getting on with your customer?

Of course it does, people like to deal with people who they like and trust but so many salespeople focus just on the like bit and try to become lifelong friends with their customers.

I remember one of my first jobs as a life insurance salesman for a massive insurance company which had thousands of salespeople in their sales teams. These people were recruited for their personality, their gift of the gab, their likeability, their affability…so that they would become liked by their customers.

Indeed this worked then but it doesn't now. Times have changed, customers have more competition to spend their money with, they have more knowledge of the products we sell from the internet and they can smell a nicey nicey salesperson a mile off.

No, building a rapport to be liked and trusted is deeper.

Begin Mirroring with the Handshake

We mostly all shake hands with our customers. Of course we do, but do you use this as an opportunity to start calibrating your customer and begin the mirroring process?

Offer your hand by subtly moving it from your side by about 6 inches; this is a very subliminal gesture for the other person to shake your hand, but enough not to get embarrassed if they don't.

Shake and measure their pace and get in tune with their rhythm at this stage. Calibrate their pace and match it. Match their squeeze and tempo of the shake.

On the subject of tempo, continue to gauge them as a person and match their pace, energy, voice and personality. Match their language and use their words, their preferred language and style. Find out their hot buttons i.e. how they tick; know what's important to them.

Immerse Yourself in Them

Mimic no, mirror yes.

Sit down with your back to the wall if you can with nothing to distract them, say a blank wall, open up your body language, engage them with hypnotic eye contact and begin your sales induction.

You can only ever begin the selling once you have established a rapport – hypnotic selling is not about being best buddies but by changing your manner to adapt to your customer's approach.

Think like them, behave like them, speak like them, know what makes them tick and you'll then be ready for the selling. But haven't you already started selling?

Matching Voice

There's so much you can do to match a person's voice and when you're on the telephone, this is pretty much all you can match. Try to match their voice speed and tone. Do they speak high or low? Try it. It does produce a very amicable conversation between two like-minded people.

4 Voice Exercises

The following exercise should be done regularly in order to gain the benefits.

Resonance

A resonant voice gives you depth and authority alongside a richer voice. It ticks all the boxes of the modern professional expert who wishes to gain credibility quickly. Here's how to develop a resonant voice:

1. Stand or sit but hold your posture well
2. Choose a note to hum
3. Next hum it for an entire breath
4. Go low with your humming
5. Feel the vibration in your chest, learn to recognise the signs of a resonant voice
6. Repeat over again

Clarity and mouth control

Useful for fluency and expressions

1. Stand or sit but hold your posture well
2. Say a letter out loud as clear as you can, for about 10 seconds or your breath runs out
3. Move your whole mouth and accentuate your cheek muscles
4. Now do the rest of the alphabet in the same manner
5. Repeat the alphabet

Quick clarity

This is a quick exercise to do when you haven't much time

1. Say the letters QEQR
2. Move your whole mouth and accentuate your cheek muscles

Developing intonation

1. If you have children, read a character book and put on some accents
2. If you don't have children, grab a company brochure and read it as though you were talking to a child. Make it interesting.

Get Off Your Ego

This week I was teaching some salespeople to build rapport and we stumbled across the topic of matching and mirroring. My group pushed back on me and explained that they'd been taught all of that before and found it quite patronising.

They felt it was too basic, and that copying someone's body language and imitating their voice was condescending to their customers.

They had a very well made point and I could see where they were coming from. And within 5 minutes, they had a realisation. Let me explain what happened to them. You might find it useful yourself.

I've always been fascinated by hypnosis and adore watching TV hypnotists like Paul McKenna, Derren Brown and Kenny Craig, aka Matt Lucas. I also trained as a hypnotist in my Master NLP Training. (Not a lot of people know that)

Hypnosis is very useful in sales -- actually incredibly useful in sales and few of my training groups know that I'm teaching them hypnotic selling skills. Would they run a mile if they knew? Instead, I call it "selling under the radar" -- it just sounds cooler.

But back to the subject of matching, let me explain how Joe Vitale explains it and it'll make absolute sense to you just as it did with my group.

Joe in his book "Buying Trances" talks about egos. Buy the way, it's a great book, you might buy it. Joe says that everyone has egos, some bigger than others. And all my life I've met salespeople with egos -- it goes with the trade -- and some argue that it is an essential trait of salespeople. I don't know I totally agree with this, but they have a point.

Please let me continue.

NLP teaches us to match our customer to get on their wavelength because people like to deal with people who are like themselves and this is true. But simply matching body language, gestures, voice, language is quite frankly, demeaning. Who's frank?

No, it's deeper than this, but not complicated. Fret not, I'm not going to wallow in theory here, that's often the problem with this sort of thing.

I have an ego -- just ask my wife... and you have one too. We all have one, even our customers. To a degree they're important things, they give us self-confidence (sometimes too much), assuredness and self-esteem. All good things. But if you get stuck in your ego, you're doomed. We all need to come out of our egos.

And when I explained this to my sales group, they didn't know how to do it, but they do really. Do you?

And when you're out of your ego, you just need to go into your customer's, because they'll have one, too. And when you're in their ego, see where they are, become like them, think like them, understand them, hear them, enter their ego.

Then you're in rapport.

So the secret is to accept that our egos are not that important -- theirs is. I promised I wouldn't wallow in theory. This is really quite simple and simple things in life are the best... just ask my wife.

Sharing the Love

Interesting title and a really useful influencing technique. It works by associating yourself with someone else who already has something about them that you would like to "borrow".

In 1997, in the aftermath of Princess Diana's tragic death, the Royal Family's reputation amongst the British public was at an all-time low. Prime Minister Tony Blair, however, had enormous popularity having just won a landslide election earlier in the year.

He decided to help Prince Charles by "lending" him his popularity. In a TV interview shortly after the accident, he was clearly seen associating with Prince Charles' mannerisms. Touching his cuff several times, standing like Prince Charles and generally mimicking him. It worked. The public associated Tony's popularity with Charles and their fondness for our prince heightened from that moment.

Last year, I found myself in China, running a week long sales conference for salespeople. The conference closed on the Friday afternoon and we enjoyed the Chinese President of the company delivering a speech. He was excellent, the audience clearly loved him. I was due up next to make a farewell speech.

So I associated myself with the President. Why not, no-one knew my techniques. I stood in the exact place as the President, used a hand microphone which he used, where normally I would use a lapel mike. I mirrored his gestures and the manner in which he stood and smiled more because he did.

My farewell speech went down well, maybe because the audience associated me with their President.

You can try this too. It's about influencing subtly, elegantly and successfully.

How to Build Rapport in 90 Seconds on a Bank Counter

Have you heard of the 90:90 rule?

It's a dinky little rule which helps bank counter staff all over the world perform better in their job.

In the first 90 seconds of meeting you, your customer will create a first impression of you and your company that will last 90% over time. Only 10% of that first impression ever changes.

So when selling on the bank counter you need to make the most of those first 90 seconds. Coming up in the next 90 seconds of your reading will be dozens of tips to help you do just that. Starting from the moment your customer appears at the till:

"Good morning, how are you today?"

Listen very carefully to the response but not just the words, observe, listen and react.

Quickly assess how much energy your customer is oozing. Are they a Speedy Gonzalez type or a slow tortoise? As soon as you've calibrated their speed, match it. Slow down or speed up to match your customer.

Smile with your customer and engage in eye contact straight away. Smiling releases those lovely free endorphins which energise your whole body and draw people towards you. Smiling also enlivens your voice.

Eye contact shows you're human and to be trusted.

Take care with your eye contact – don't stare. Be aware of how often you blink. To prevent a staring gaze, try to blink more often. Also develop a natural gaze, not a fixed look. Many people lock onto one eye or a spot on their nose but the trick is to gaze at the customer's face. Start looking at one eye, slowly move to the next and then to the mouth in a triangular fashion. This gaze is very welcoming, warm and friendly.

As you listen to your customer tell you about their day or give you their instruction, move your head backwards an inch or two. This is a non-aggressive gesture and creates a good impression. At the same time tilt your head slightly to one side – not too much – just enough to lower your height by a centimetre. Again this is a non-aggressive gesture designed to lower your customer's guard towards you as a person.

These little techniques do work – try them.

A final head gesture is to show that you're thinking through their request by looking up slightly away from their eye contact before returning to their eyes. This is a brilliant signal which shows that you're thinking.

Naturally you should be using their name now if they have given you any paper, passbook or card. And your computer system will quickly show you all the dealings your company should you need this.

But we're still in the first 90 seconds.

Now engage in some conversation. This is very difficult especially when it's busy, or you have a glass screen or the customer doesn't want to talk and is in a hurry. That's fine but you should try.

Learn to multi task. I know we men find this terribly difficult and you ladies find it so very easy. But we men must learn to carry out the transaction requested by the customer effortlessly and as second nature so we can focus on some conversation. We want to do this because we'd like the opportunity to introduce some of our products to our customer.

As you talk or ask questions be aware of the customer's voice pitch and pace and try to match this as accurately as you can. Maybe a slightly lower voice would be closer to your customer's and if they speak slowly, then you should slow down a tad as well.

Break the ice somehow. Someone I know who has worked on the counter for years, always has a funny pen top – like a cuddly toy or a plastic face – and this alone draws the customer's attention.

Find something in common with the customer. Here in the UK, we just love to talk about the weather – it gets most people talking.

Maybe something exciting is happening in town. For example the town fun run begins on Saturday so ask the customer if they've been in training. Say it with a smile and it might get them chuckling.

Here's a great tip for you. What is it that both you and every customer have in common? That's right….the company you work for: Mid-West Building Society. So ask them:

- "How have you found us over the years?"
- "What sort of changes have you seen over the last few years?"
- "Why do you like coming back to us?"
- "How do you see us helping you in the future?"

Try it, it will work for you.

Something else to chat about that you might have in common with your customer is a common enemy. I don't mean terrorists or anything drastic like that, but the tax man for example, or interest rates going up, or house prices coming down. People like to rally together with a common gripe or common enemy.

That's probably about 90 seconds.

With a fabulous first impression created and rapport built nicely, you can probe a little more to see if one of your products or services might suit the customer.

Be careful of falling into the trap of flogging one product each day or having a campaign for this service on Wednesdays. Customers are all different. Find out a little more about them, ask some probing non aggressive questions, and you'll reveal some needs that you could use to match against your products.

90 seconds is not long. Probably how long it took you to read this article but please don't underestimate the power of the 90:90 rule when serving customers at the counter. Remember the first 90 seconds is when they create a lasting impression that will stick 90% over time.

A Unique Rapport Building Technique

I'm going to combine two very clever techniques from NLP into one mesmerising simple tactic to influence someone.

Let me explain how.

One of the quickest ways to gain rapport with someone is to offer a compliment. Something genuine and meaningful. This has been reported well before NLP was even mentioned; Dale Carnegie mentioned it in his book in the early 20th century.

Earlier this year I was working in Dubai for a bank and helping their sales advisers become even more effective in selling. One man was presenting in the classroom and I particularly liked his jacket. It was a local design. A shalwar waistcoat. I thought it was elegant, very tasteful and fitted the occasion.

I genuinely thought so and later bought one in the shopping mall.

At the time I complimented him and said how handsome it made him look. He "purred".

And at the same time I went to touch his shoulder as this is an anchor which I wanted to associate with the moment for him.

The whole group warmed to me and we enjoyed the rest of our time together. As we all departed the training my new friend came up to shake my hand. As I did so I touched his shoulder once more, re-igniting the compliment and the warm feeling he had from earlier. He smiled like a Cheshire cat and we are now friends on Facebook and Linked in contacts.

So combine a compliment with a subtle touch anchor to cement the moment and bring it back just by firing the anchor later.

Don't Forget Common Ground

One of the advantages of your favourite Premiere League Football team playing erratically is that you can buy tickets for home matches. And so this happened for me at Manchester United's Old Trafford ground.

With my two teenage sons, we ventured to Manchester with our tickets for the first time. Unfortunately we were unable to secure three consecutive seats, my two boys sat next to each other but I was a couple of seats behind them on my own.

However we were amongst fellow fans, and I soon became ensconced in conversation about Manchester United past and present with my two adjoining new friends. We spoke about Eric Cantona's brilliance, Sparky's incisiveness in attack and Bruce's staunch defensiveness. Plus Schmeichel's goal keeping antics.

We were all soon best buddies.

Doesn't it just prove the value of common ground?

I know it's a cliché, but do you still seek common ground with your customers and clients? It's one of the rapport building techniques that will live forever.

Didn't Oasis want to "live forever"?

Enough of the Manchester links, my friends in Liverpool will never let me live that down.

Client Influencing Stories

Have you ever attended a Speed Networking event? Fabulous idea, naturally, where likeminded business professionals have 2 minutes to tell each other about their services and products.

Unfortunately they can become very "samey", with everyone spouting out their value propositions and elevator pitches. We've heard it all before.

An alternative is to develop client influencing stories. These mini stories are designed to influence people on a subconscious level, to understand in under a minute, exactly what value you provide to your clients.

The secret is to keep them to a minute and to follow the age old steps to crafting the story. Let me give you an example, then I'll unpack what I did.

Colin and Debi

Colin was a hard worker, totally dedicated to his young wife Debi. He was a railway worker eagerly completing his apprenticeship. He had ambitions to be a train driver and was looking forward to starting a family as soon as they could afford to.

Debi and Colin were in their early 20s, newly married, and that day, were celebrating their first year's wedding anniversary. It was a cold November day, Colin was working late, keen to get home for Debi's surprise meal, which he knew about, after all, Debi had given him a huge number of hints. Colin was tall, over 6 feet, strong and totally in love.

The evening fog had descended on the rail yard, Colin's last job that evening was to guide two locomotives into the sidings, couple them together and then get off for home.

He used a night light system designed to give train drivers instructions on the same basis as traffic lights. Colin was experienced in this procedure and had just indicated to the first driver to hold still whilst he crossed the tracks to show the second driver to begin coming forward.

Whether the first driver hadn't seen the light or he was half asleep, was irrelevant as the solid steel coupling device took the life out of Colin instantly.

One year later, Debi had begun to socialise once again and had returned to work on a part-time basis, not for the money, but for the need to continue her life. The life assurance policy I'd sold them paid off their mortgage completely and gave Debi a lump sum that gave her the ability to never worry about money again and to rebuild her life.

The 4 Steps To Follow

A true story which occurred early in my career as a life assurance salesperson, and yes, I've told the story many times.

The story clearly lays out the value I provided at the time to customers, mixes emotions with visual imagination and can be told in under one minute.

It follows these steps:

3. Scene and characters
4. Journey
5. Obstacle
6. Solution

Can you recall the character Colin? And the scene? Late November, happy married young couple, 6 foot tall Colin.

The journey…coupling the trains in the foggy evening. The obstacle…coupling successfully so he could return home for a romantic meal.

The solution…life assurance that allowed Debi never to worry about money again.

Story Uses

The client influencing story has many uses. You can use them with customers when you want to influence them to take out a product, or introduce the value you provide. You can also use them with your introducers.

Many of my clients rely on bank or building society staff to provide leads and telling these stories to them is a powerful way of illustrating what you do.

People remember emotions and can imagine the scene, so powerful in influencing them.

Wouldn't they also be useful when speed networking as well? It would certainly prevent the yawns.

How to Ooze Empathy

NLP's Perceptual Positions

I had never travelled on a rollercoaster. Honest, I know it sounds remarkable, but I never had the courage to climb in the small cab and ride the heart-wrenching and stomach-churning experience.

Until... one afternoon over Christmas when my youngest son dared me to get on the ride at Poulton's Park. Now if you ever want to motivate me to do something, you only need to dare me. I think it's hard wired into most men.

I watched Euan first and thought I'd use the 1st, 2nd, 3rd position that we use all the time when selling. Now this clever little tip helps, you see, to feel and fully understand what it's like for someone else and in sales, this is quite a useful way of exploring the customer's point of view.

1st position

1st position is where you look at things through your own eyes and as I stared at Euan on the rollercoaster, all I could think of was fear, trepidation -- how foolish, help!

2nd position

2nd position is where you step out of your shoes and move into the customer's shoes and look at things through this person's eyes -- in other words, see and feel their point of view. So I tried this and moved into Euan's shoes. Initially I could still feel my fear and trepidation, but I kept at it and began to see how Euan saw the ride. He was smiling and cheering, so loud I could hear him from where I was standing. As he approached the top of the loop just before he was to plunge downwards at breath-taking speed, his look was of apprehension, but total excitement. He was enjoying the thrill of the ride and I started to feel what this was like for him.

3rd position

3rd position is where you stand back, disassociate yourself from both viewpoints and look objectively at the situation. With customers, we get to see their views and ours in tandem. On the rollercoaster, I could see Euan's viewpoint, mine and the other passengers on the coaster. I realised that everyone seemed to be having fun and that this miserable father was seeing the rollercoaster in a very blinkered way.

And did I enjoy it? Yes I did, and I had to go on it again and again. In fact, since it wasn't too busy, I went on the same ride 3 times and Euan now thinks his Dad is really cool.

So next time you really want to appreciate your customer's point of view, go from 1st position, to 2nd and then finally to 3rd position.

Walking in Your Customer's Shoes

I have two sons separated by 2 years, very similar in looks but you couldn't get two more different characters. One is reserved, effortlessly sensitive, worries about people all the time and can spot a personal feeling a mile away even in camouflage.

My other son is completely oblivious to people's feelings, beliefs and opinions and is always the centre of attention and very talkative. Not that he's a bad boy, he's just different.

I know which one is going to be the natural salesperson.

You see salespeople, coaches, team leaders, sales support teams all need to be sensitive to other people's situations, they need to show empathy to customer's positions in order to gain rapport and sell successfully. Empathy can be defined as knowing how people think, what's going on in their world without necessarily agreeing with them. And I firmly believe that this skill can be learnt, so there is hope for my son.

There are two steps to having empathy with customers:

1. Step one is being aware of their situation.
2. Step two is acknowledging that you are aware.

Remember to go to step two as people can't guess that you understand them; you have to make it known.

Here are some practical tips to turn up your empathy volume by being aware of their situation and then showing that you're responsive.

Read between the lines

I call this level 3 or global listening – it's the ability to read what's not been said, to rely on gut reactions, to use your sixth sense, to use your intuition. That way you can understand where the customer is coming from. Level 1 and 2 listening is as far as most of us go – level 1 is selfish listening in that everything you hear gets related to your personal experiences and for your own purposes. Level 2 is listening or active listening and appreciating your customer's point of view.

Trust your level 3. Trust your intuition to read between the lines.

Non-verbal clues

Or body language. To be really empathetic you need to be able to read body language so you can read beyond what is being said. People can change the words they use but they can't hide their body language. Look for clusters of gestures, not isolated ones.

For example crossed arms might be because they're cold or are hiding their paunch. It may not mean being negative or hostile. But crossed arms, alongside crossed body and legs, sitting behind a barrier, jerky eye contact and pacier language would normally mean there's something up in their mind, and it's not good.

Lower your voice tone

A lower voice pitch is more empathetic. Learn to deepen your tone and people will warm to you sooner. Do ensure your vocals have a good range though; no one wants to listen to someone who is monotone in their delivery.

Listen more

Most salespeople appreciate this but three things you can do to listen with empathy is to paraphrase, mirror language and use silence more. Paraphrasing asks that you use the customer's language and words when summarising. Occasionally repeat back one or two words and raise your voice as you say them to indicate a subtle question. This will get the customer to say more. And silence is the best way to let your customer say how it is, especially on the phone. I always believe that phone operators would become comfortable with a few seconds of silence so long as there is a purpose to this.

Tell stories

Tell stories during your selling. Use stories to prove your expertise, to demonstrate your product's uniqueness, in fact any part of the sales process can be enlivened with a story. Now when you tell a story, a strange thing happens in the customer's mind. They translate the story into their world as if they were in the story. This helps to show them that you are like them, you share similar ideals. People love a story, it's something granted to us as children and we never lose the irresistibility of a tale.

Empathy gestures

Showing empathy with your body language is something that women are far better at than men. My daughter, who is 8 next month, has this completely tied up. She knows when to turn on the empathy charm with Daddy to get what she wants. One of her weapons is the head tilt. Bethan uses this when she wants to show lots of empathy with my situation and simply tilts her head sideways. This has a magical effect on the person talking and shows deep empathy.

Try this yourself.

Other empathy creating gestures are smiles, eye contact, open body language, hands to face to indicate deep listening and thinking about your situation.

Reflective statements

These are really useful little phrases that tell your customer that you see where they're coming from. You may not necessarily agree with them but you appreciate their point of view. That's empathy and not being a "yes" man or woman. Some examples:

"I understand what you're saying."

"I can appreciate how you feel about that."

"I've been through that as well and it was terrible."

"I see where you're coming from."

"Gosh, that must be awful."

So there we have my 9 tips to show more empathy with your customer – a particularly important skill for salespeople or anyone who deals with people as part of their profession. Some people are natural at it – most of us have to learn it though – these 9 tips can help you do just that.

Are you Brexit or Bremain?

And how this can help you empathise more with your customers.

The vote is going to be very close, closer than our current political leaders dare to admit. The British reject the continual political control that membership of the EU gives us; we love the trade and the wealth but despise the directives coming out of Brussels and the drive towards ever closer political union.

We have these views because we're being selfish in part, we're only looking at the situation in our own "shoes". Let me explain further.

NLP gives us the 3 perceptual positions. Position one is where we only see things from our point of view, position two is where we can climb into the customer's shoes and see things from their point of view, associate with them deeply. Position three is where we disassociate ourselves from both our shoes and the customer's and see both points of view.

Back to the issue of Europe and membership. Let's try and see things from our European partners' point of view. Every single member except the UK, has in the last hundred years, been invaded and controlled by another state. Think about it, they all have at some point, except us. So after the second world war, the two largest states – France and West Germany – got together to try to prevent future wars and came up with the EU in the 1950s.

Originally a trade body brought them together but they yearned for complete political joint control to ensure a war never ever happens again in Europe.

Fine intentions. Political union gives them security and stability and this is driving them forward towards that goal.

But it's not our goal. We haven't been invaded since 1066 and have no understanding of being occupied and told what to do by another state.

I wish someone would see it from perceptual position three – both sides, and come up with an agreement we can both live with. I believe our present PM is aiming to do that and I'll be voting Bremain. What about you?

The Empathetic Conversation Cycle

Many roles of the salesperson and their manager involve asking questions. Coaching sessions, factfinding customer needs, establishing situations, one to one meetings…the list goes on. We're all taught questioning techniques to enhance the conversation – open versus closed versus hypothetical and so on.

But I still witness a lot of one sided interrogations. On the face of it, really good questions being used, and first class listening skills being deployed. Yet I still see an interrogation.

There's lots of ways to avoid this scenario, my favourite is to deploy the conversation cycle. Let me explain how this works.

A typical questioning session involves person A asking the question, person B answering it, person A following up with another question and person B answering. Nothing wrong with that approach but it isn't a conversation. Conversations swing back and forth and can continue for ages. Let's mash this up a bit.

Person A still asks a question and you can do all the sugar coating and softening you like with this question, make it a high gain, curious open question if you want, and person B still answers it. But this time person A does some form of acknowledging to encourage more response from person B.

This can be:

- A verbal nod such as "I see", "That's fascinating", or "Keep going".
- An empathy statement which shows you've experienced just the same thing. A "me too" moment. For example person B might answer the question about their holiday in Florida when they swam with the dolphins. Person A would empathise with "We holidayed in Florida last year and the weather was fantastic, but we didn't get to that theme park. It sounds fun."
- A reflective statement such as "Swimming with dolphins must have been an amazing experience".

Now these acknowledgements turn things around immensely. The aim is to allow person B to carry on talking and conversation can ensue quite quickly. But let me finish off the cycle in style for you and add a fourth element.

So person A asks a question, person B is kind enough to respond, person A then throws in an acknowledgement, person B doesn't respond, so person A throws in an "inform".

An "inform" is merely a statement, a precursor to another question. Some new context in order to launch the next phase of the conversation. It allows you to steer the conversation in the direction you seek. For example, following our dolphin story.

Person A might acknowledge and say how fascinating that must have been and might add "Holidays are an important expenditure for us all, and many client spend a fair proportion of their disposable income on leisure and holidays."

That's the "inform" – the context to launch another question such as "What proportion of your disposable income do you like to allocate to leisure activities?"

So that's the cycle:

And you can go back and forth, sideways, around the cycle…there are no rules on that, just enjoy a good conversation rather than an interrogation.

Tuning Your Listening to the Next Level

"Daddy, are you listening to me?" This sent me spluttering over my cornflakes and drizzling milk down my freshly ironed shirt. "I'm listening Bethan, honest", knowing full well that I was merely looking at my daughter and hadn't followed a word she was saying.

Shame on you Daddy.

"Sorry Bethan, what did you say?"

"It doesn't matter now, Daddy."

Gone forever that conversation and my daughter sulked for the rest of the breakfast. All because I simply hadn't listened. I got stuck in my own little world relating everything to me and my concerns. Although I was carrying out classic active listening gestures – you know, eye contact, face tilt, nodding, those little "uh huhs", I wasn't really listening.

But a woman is better skilled than us men at communicating – that's been proven time and time again. And my daughter, at only 5, can spot when a man isn't listening properly.

OK, I kind of got away with it this morning over breakfast... I think... I'll wait until tonight to see if Bethan is still talking to me. But in sales you won't get away with it, you'll lose the sale and that's not so good. Imagine if your customer turned round to you and said, "You're not really listening to me, are you?"

That would be a killer, wouldn't it?

When practising rapport selling, not listening properly is practically a hanging offence. So how do we really do this? Two things.

One. Kick out active listening techniques. They don't work. They're false because just by giving the impression that you're listening doesn't add up. My daughter saw straight through me this morning and your customer will, too.

Two. Just know that listening is hard work and you have to concentrate on it. Someone once said to me many years ago that listening is really tough. At the time, I thought this was nonsense and argued that talking was harder. How could I have been so wrong? You have to literally concentrate on listening to get it right.

And when you do, the rewards are immense in selling. You build a rapport quickly, you find out about your customer – their needs, wants, desires, criteria – their problems and concerns. You know when to give benefits, you know when there's a customer concern coming up, you know when to close. And these things add up to selling.

So how do we do it? Think 3 levels of listening – a bit like a volume control on your IPod.

When you want to listen more, just turn up your volume control. I know it sounds a little bit daft, but I have this imaginary volume control in my head and when I'm selling or consulting with clients and I want to turn up my listening, I turn up my volume control and this tells my brain to start listening more.

My volume control has three levels – level one, two and three.

So let me tell you about these.

Level 1 Listening

Level 1 listening or internal listening is when we are listening to sounds and information around us that are just for our purposes and no one else. I recall September 11th and having to use Edinburgh airport to fly home. Great timing on my part, eh? The airport was in chaos. There were security checks everywhere, people shouting and panicking – it was a nightmare.

There I was, fully aware of what was going on and intent on getting home safely and on time. I was in level 1 listening mode and I didn't care about anyone else. I just wanted to hear the information and sounds that would mean that I got home. I listened out for the broadcasts and particularly the word Birmingham. I kept my ears open for information that would help me and no one else.

When people talk to you, do you relate what they are saying to your experience? When someone told you they went skiing this year, did you immediately relate this to your last skiing holiday and talk about that? We've all done it, haven't we? Inadvertently, we're level 1 listening and thinking only of ourselves.

At level 1, our attention is on ourselves. We listen to the words of the other person, but the focus is on what it means to us. At level 1 the spotlight is on me – my thoughts, my judgments, my feelings, my conclusions about myself and others.

Have you ever been thinking about what you are going to say next? We all do this.

So turn up your volume control now to level 2 and feel the difference.

Level 2 Listening

Level 2 listening or focused listening comes next.

At level 2 there is a sharp focus on the other person. You can see it in people's posture when they are communicating at level 2. Probably both leaning forward, looking intently at each other. There is a great deal of attention on the other person and not much awareness of the outside world.

You are beginning to see their words and reasoning on their side of the fence. You've put yourself in their shoes and in their world. The next time someone tells you about their holiday, relate their experiences to them. How they saw it, what they encountered, what feelings of excitement they had.

Your awareness is totally on the other person. You listen for their words, their expression, their emotion, everything they bring. You notice what they say, how they say it. You notice what they don't say. You see how they smile or hear the tears in their voice. You listen for what they value. You listen for their vision and what makes them energetic.

You switch off all distractions (and I know this can be difficult).

I remember one of my first sales jobs selling mortgages to clients of an estate agency in Guildford High Street. My desk was right bang in the front office by the door – not ideal. And if you want to see big windows, you only have to go as far as your nearest estate agents.

The distractions were enormous as we were on the main shopping street in town.

But you need to tune out all distractions and focus just on your client to be successful at level 2.

Now turn up your volume control to the maximum – level 3.

Level 3 Listening

Level 3 listening or global listening is the ultimate Rapport Seller's skill.

At Level 3, you listen at 360 degrees. In fact, you listen as though you and the client were at the centre of the universe receiving information from everywhere at once. Level 3 includes everything you can observe with your senses: what you see, hear, smell, and feel – the tactile sensations as well as the atmosphere.

If Level 2 is an old dial up modem, Level 3 is wireless broadband with no physical connections -- just a room full of digital signals. We can't see these signals, but we know they're there. Level 3 uses these invisible signals.

My wife is great at level 3 listening – in fact, research suggests that women are better at this than men.

Some wonderful research was conducted by Allan and Barbara Pease and published in their book "Why Men Don't Listen and Women Can't Read Maps". Do buy it and enjoy over Christmas. Very light, very funny and very revealing.

For many people this is a new realm of listening. One of the benefits of learning to listen at Level 3 is greater access to your intuition. From your intuition you receive information that is not directly observable, and you use that information just as you'd use words coming from the client's mouth. At Level 3, intuition is simply more information.

Next time, just try your level 3. Trust your intuition, your gut reaction, your sixth sense to hear what is not visibly there.

And next time I'm at the breakfast table stuck in my own little world listening to my daughter at level 1, I'll just have to turn up my imaginary volume control and listen to level 3 and see the difference in her beautiful sparkling blue eyes.

A Day in the Life of Your Customer

One of my favourite all time tunes is "A Day in the Life" by The Beatles. It recalls the tripped out day that both Paul McCartney and John Lennon had. While Lennon's lyrics were inspired by contemporary newspaper articles, McCartney's lyrics were based on reminiscences about his youth. It was a day in the life.

This is something we need to do for our customers. The ultimate empathy test. Since they're now in full control of the buying and we just facilitate that, we need to have an understanding as to how they buy, so imagine a day in the life of your buyer.

So, for example, say you sell mortgages and protection to help people secure their home.

Where does your customer go, what sites do they search, what words do they put into the search engines? Who do they talk to, which social network do they use most to see recommendations, which aggregator sites attract them? And so on.

Next you devise a sales process that merely helps them along the way. Provide online materials to give them the answers they need, provide information in the form of videos and let them find you and connect with you in the way they prefer.

For example, we sell an online package that helps people pass a particular mortgage exam. We sell it online with no human interaction at all. Our potential customers go online and search with Google and visit YouTube, online forums and Facebook. And I know they like to get things for free.

So we pay Google some money for pay per click advertising using specific keywords; this brings them to our various sites. On YouTube we have a number of free videos which answer all their questions. People searching for the exams often want to know how to get into the mortgage sector which is incredibly regulated. So we answer these questions on videos, lots of them, recorded by me. We have free email lists where they can get a free question sent every day. On Facebook we have articles and videos helping people to sell, these all link back to our websites where we have an online credit card acceptance. We also take PayPal because 75% of our customers prefer this. Plus an email contact with which they can ask any question they like.

We've spent a Day in the Life of our customers. Have you done this recently?

If I were selling mortgages, I would do everything listed above but would allow them the facility to speak with me online using video and conduct the whole mortgage meeting process via online methods, because that's how customers now want to buy. But you may think differently, it all depends on the day in the life of your customer.

And the Beatles number was ranked the 28th greatest song of all time by Rolling Stone magazine.

Spotting Thinking Styles

The eyes have it

Plenty of conclusive research shows that when someone is accessing their minds for information, really thinking about it, their eyes will move in a certain direction.

Upwards for pictures, sideways for sounds and words, down right for feelings and down left when talking to themselves. It's important to realise that the thinking has to be fairly deep. A generalisation from the person will not reveal any eye movement, as the answer was pretty much instantaneous. In these situations you get that look straight at you.

Let's have a look at each set of eye movements.

Visual Eye Movements

When people are thinking of a picture in their heads, they will look upwards often with a tilt of the head. If you want to get scientific, if someone looks up to their right, they are creating a picture in the head. But if someone is recalling a picture from their memory, they'll look up to their left. Tricky to remember which is which sometimes, so just look for an upwards glance.

Let's summarise with a picture. You are looking at this person:

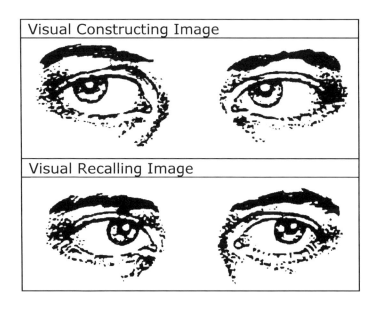

Auditory Eye Movement

Auditory preferred people will look sideways. To their right for creating sounds or conversations, to their left for recalling a sound.

Here's the picture. Remember you are looking at this person.

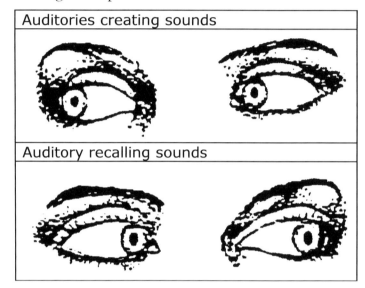

Auditories creating sounds

Auditory recalling sounds

Kinaesthetic Eye Movement

These people will have eye movements generally down to their right. They are accessing a notion, a feeling, a gut reaction…something to make them feel right or wrong or good or bad about something that's on their mind. Down right is the direction of their eyes.

Seen visually as this:

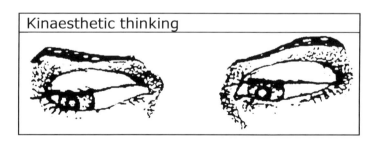

Kinaesthetic thinking

Auditory Digital Eye Movement

When you spot an auditory digital person looking down to their left, they are talking to themselves.

Interrupt them at your peril.

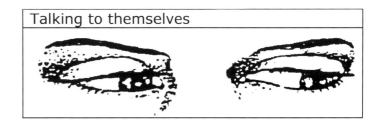

Talking to themselves

Summary of Eye Movements

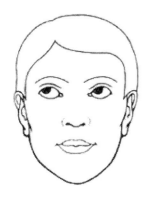

Visual Constructed

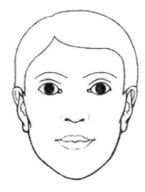

Visual Defocussed

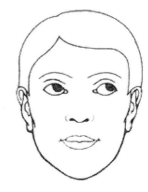

Visual Remembered

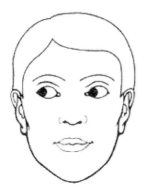

Auditory Constructed

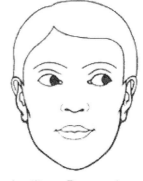

Auditory Remembered

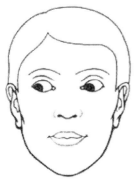

Kinaesthetic

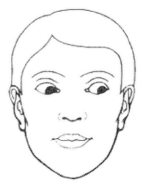

Auditory Digital

Practicing the Eyes

The following is an exercise you can carry out with a partner to practise and master the technique.

Sit facing each other and take in turns to ask the other person the following questions. They are designed to allow the eyes to move in the directions we talked about. The person who answers the questions must relax and really think about the answers. Watch their eyes closely, they should move in the direction of the diagram.

Visual Remembered	How many windows are there in your house? What did your first school look like? Which of your friends has the longest hair?	
Visual Constructed	What would you look like dressed as an Eskimo? Imagine a policeman in a suit of armour. What would an orange elephant with two trunks look like?	
Auditory Remembered	What does your alarm clock sound like? What was your favourite song as a youngster? What is your favourite sound from nature?	
Auditory constructed	What would I sound like with Donald Duck's voice? What was the last thing I said? What was the last thing you heard on leaving your house today?	

Kino	Which carpet in your house is the softest? Imagine walking barefoot in the sand. How cold was the sea last time you felt it?	
Auditory Digital	List the steps you took to arrive here this morning. Mull it over right now, but where would be your favourite holiday destination? Explain how you would change a tyre on a car.	

Reframing in Sales

Reframe the Pressure

Pressure comes from a variety of sources in sales and I've seen it countless times in salespeople.

And how do we handle it? Some handle it really well, a few thrive on it, but for most of us mere mortals we need some strategies to deal with it. Here's a useful technique to help you do just that.

Put a big square in your head which represents your thoughts.

Divide the square into 4.

The top two squares are for future thoughts, in other words, thoughts that relate to future happenings, future thinking. The bottom two are past thoughts – things that have already happened – it's good to forget these once you've learnt from them.

Today I want to focus on the top two boxes – future thinking.

The left hand box is for bad future thinking and the right hand box is for good future thinking. For example bad thinking might be worrying about things, targets not being met or not being able to pay the mortgage. Future good thoughts might be your holiday coming up or receiving a big fat bonus or just relaxing at the weekend.

Here's the secret. When you have some pressure and the resulting thought is going to be future bad, just move it physically into the other box, future good and reframe it. And then see what it looks like then.

Here's some examples:

- No sale yet today becomes only a matter of time for my next sale.
- Worrying about the economy becomes excited about future opportunities.
- Pressure to succeed from my boss becomes an opportunity to shine when I succeed.
- Too light a sales pipeline becomes there's always going to be new business if I just carry on prospecting for it.
- If I don't meet that deadline becomes when I do it's going to be a great success.

By constantly moving your thoughts from the top left to the top right, will foster a positive feast type of attitude because you know things will come good in the end.

Now you have a strategy to handle constant pressure, but just don't tell anyone what you're doing, remember it's your mind and you can do whatever you want inside it.

You Think You're Under Pressure at Work?

A cold November morning in Essex. Industrial park. Myriad of offices putting car parking under pressure so everyone stations their cars along the side of roads making passing impossible and putting side mirrors in jeopardy of their lives.

Enter a 42 tonne articulated lorry from Boston, Lincolnshire. Obviously been on the road since the early hours, a very young looking driver with a green polo shirt advertising his company's brand.

The only way into the entrance to the cul-de-sac of warehouses was backwards.

Cool as a cucumber, he reversed this monstrous truck into the tiny entrance with an audience of cars, trucks and onlookers.

Talk about pressure.

And the boy came good. He reversed perfectly and I took a photo of his calm demeanour.

So if you think you're under pressure and it's affecting your output, think again. There's always someone else worse off than you. We need to put pressure into perspective.

Pre-Frame Your Objections

You never win an argument with a customer but I have witnessed it, seen it many times, when salespeople are taught to overcome objections during the close phase. This is old fashioned as well as unproductive.

The trick is to pre-empt the objection earlier in the meeting. Head it off at the pass. Close the open doors.

However, salespeople tell me that they don't know which one to pre-empt as customers always baulk at something different.

Here's the answer.

There are only 4 objections and these encompass every variation. The customer:

1.   Has no time
2.   Has no money or can't afford it
3.   Doesn't believe you
4.   Does believe you but doesn't think it'll work for them

So think of a way to pre-empt these before they rear their ugly head, because they invariably will.

Right now you're throwing all sorts of objections at me to see if they fit the 4 categories, but I guarantee every single one you tell me fits under one of them.

How to Reframe Customer Objections

Modern salespeople, like you, ensure that typical reservations are eliminated during the sales process and not left to the end. Do that and you realise quickly that you never win an argument with a customer. Using the NLP's reframe tool can ensure that when you do have to handle a reservation or two, it's elegant and successful.

Here's how.

1.   Pace the objection
2.   Reveal their intentions
3.   Reframe the content or context

Pacing the objection merely involves catching up with the customer on exactly what they mean. Listen to them, paraphrase what they're saying, empathise with them and probe a little more to uncover it. Once you've paced them, you then reveal their intentions. Here you need to see their frame, in other words how they see the issue

Why are they asking the question or posing the concern? Are they genuinely just wanting more information or are they throwing up a smoke screen to avoid having to say "no"? This is why we need to discover the intentions. Keep an eye out for any incongruence in their physiology. Compare how they appear and sound to when you first calibrated them, is there any leakage? If so, probe; "Is there anything else on your mind?"

If their intention is curiosity to discover more or they genuinely have an issue, then clarify the information. If they understand but don't like something, then reframe it. Reframe the context of their concern, for example, if they think it's rather expensive, then enquire what they are comparing it to in their minds. This morning I was on the phone to a potential new corporate client. We happened to talk price, I gave him an indication, and he went very quiet at that point. I asked him what he was comparing this to and he mentioned that the franchise motor company provided the training at a fraction of my cost, so he wasn't ready for my fee.

Reframing the content could involve you piling on more value and benefits so they see that the price brings them value.

So there we have objection handling using the reframe tool. Quite frankly, it's a most elegant approach.

Framing Your Sales Success

Before I start this section, let me tell you that I'm going to give you a little known trade secret.

Ok, let's start. You know I'm a really big fan of NLP in sales. Of course you can get jabs for NLP at the chemists.

But rid yourself of the mystique surrounding it and you have a really practical set of tools to use as a salesperson or coach.

One of my favourites is framing.

Let me explain how this will make a difference to how you sell.

Everything has a context, a topic surrounding the event. It might be a sales situation, a coaching event, a training course. Your customer or coachee is stuck in the frame and you can't blame them because that's where they are.

Now the frame might be the closing segment of the sales meeting where the customer has to make a decision. Or the coaching event where the salesperson needs to give you their thoughts about how the sales call went.

If the outcome doesn't go your way, you can try to re-frame the situation but this is quite challenging at the best of times. This is why objection handling at the close is so dangerous and unpleasant or begging the salesperson to give you some sort of opinion of the sales meeting following your first request.

The secret here is to pre-frame beforehand.

For objection handling, you pre-empt any problems before they become problems, but I think we already know this. If your product is pricy, make sure you justify this extra cost very early on. If it only comes in black, then give a valuable reason why. If your customers don't like buying protection policies from you after they've secured a mortgage deal from you, then bring the subject up before you mention mortgage and secure the sale there and then.

If your coachee is reticent to give you their opinions, tell them that's what you expect and explain the advantages of doing so even before you start the coaching session.

This is well known and documented, but here's a little secret you won't have heard of.

Before the frame starts with your customer, make a request, then start the frame.

If it's a sales meeting say something like:

"Before we start our mortgage discussion, may I ask how important it is to know that you can keep your home if anything is thrown at you that might make you lose it, such as fire, flood, death of your partner?"

"OK, before we start our coaching session do you mind me asking if you are more motivated if I tell you what to do or if you figure it out yourself?"

The psychology is that "before we start" catches them off guard as they haven't started the formal part, the frame. So they'll often give way to your request or give you an unguarded answer. You've successfully pre-framed the situation and made your life easier later on.

Try it, it does work. Did you notice I used it with you at the beginning of this section?

Provocative Objection Handling

Handling customer reservations does rather smack of 1990s selling techniques. I prefer to deal with the problems and issues earlier on rather than at the end. This technique works whether you're selling a product or an idea. You probably know what the issues are going to be, so raise them early and deal with them then.

But occasionally a lingering problem might rear its head once you've asked for the order or proposed your idea to the customer.

If so, try provocative objection handling, it might just work.

Let me explain.

They throw up a problem or barrier. Instead of dealing with it, don't. Just say something like: "Do you know perhaps you're just not right for this idea, just not ready. It's OK, this idea is not for everyone and maybe it's not for you."

Now wait for a reaction. They'll respond quickly and probably tell you that everything else is fine about the idea. Now they're on the back foot and will defend the fact that they are right for the idea.

It does work. It uses the Cialdini influencing principle of scarcity.

And if it doesn't… then maybe they weren't right for the idea or the product and you can move onto the next person. Sometimes we have nothing to lose.

NLP and Buying Signals

It was on the fourth floor in the boardroom in Mayfair on a cold November morning. My client was presenting to a small group of buyers and she'd asked me to observe and give her some feedback on her presentation skills.

She was fluent, polished, with an effective PowerPoint deck visualising the concepts, but there was one thing she hadn't noticed. The group of buyers were ready to buy. I could tell it, their body language had leaked positively (more about this shortly), their gestures had moved to a buying state. They wanted to buy and my client just continued.

Thankfully nothing was lost, however her continued presentation did spur an awkward question which she managed to salvage. If however, she had recognised they were ready to buy, her presentation would've been much quicker.

I've seen it many times where salespeople get caught up in their pitch and omit to look for buying signals. NLP can help.

Peripheral Vision

This is a technique to practise right now. Most of us use foveal vision, in other words we lock onto people's faces and eyes. This is down to our training. Still give people eye contact of course, match the same amount of eye contact they give you, build the rapport, but go peripheral.

To practise this you may wish to sit down comfortably and look at a spot on the wall in front of you. Focus on this spot and let your peripheral vision move your gaze to your left and right. Don't move your head or your focus but let the brain go peripheral. It has a relaxing side effect as well as allowing you to see all of someone rather than just their eyes.

And you need to do this for the next step – calibrate.

Calibrate

When I meet a client for the first time I'm going to take a snapshot of what they look like, sound like, their normal gestures and posture. I'm calibrating their physiology when they are relaxed, with an inquisitive state of mind maybe. I then make a mental note.

Leakage

Awful phrase, and I'm referring to physiology leakage. In other words, they've changed or leaked from how they normally look or sound. This is where you look for your next steps. NLP says that the person with the most flexibility in behaviour will win.

I have an imaginary traffic light on people's heads. Leakage causes the traffic light to change. When it's green all is well and I continue. When it's amber or green, I'll pause and enquire if there's a problem or if they have questions. Naturally I'm looking for leakage to show me their new state of mind.

Positive leakage can be:

- Slowly learning forward from a backward position
- Slow head nod
- Opening up the body, removing folded arms
- Hands to face in a thinking gesture
- Pupil dilation – you've got to be close for this
- Voice tone quickens with excitement
- Smiles and reassuring nods
- Looking through visual aids and putting them down with a smile

| **Confident** | **Superiority** | **Dissatisfied or uncomfortable** |

Holding back strong feelings and emotions

Unhappy, angry and defensive

Contended, confident and smug

Self-satisfied and pompous person

Critical evaluation

"The Thinker"

"Let me consider"

Difficulty in concluding

"What was that again?"

Needs time to conclude

"Well I don't know"

"I can't see it"

Steepling – confident and knowledgeable

Sit-down readiness

Deep in troubled thought

Hot under the collar

Worried

Nervous

People who want to consciously hide their conversation

Rubbing wet palms against a fabric communicates nervousness

Hand to chest - communicates loyalty, honesty and devotion

If you see these, or some of them, then the leakage is telling you that they may be ready to move forward, so ask them if everything is ok. For visuals ask "How is this all looking?", if auditory "How does this all sound?", for kinos "How does this feel?", for digitals "Does this all make sense?"

And if you get a positive reaction to these test closes, close.

If you would like to assess your observation of leakage here is a free resource. Head to:

https://youtu.be/gpiUohPPyks

Watch the video and then you should go to the online questionnaire which can be completed and your results will be available immediately. Very interesting indeed.

There's a Tell For Everything

Earlier this year I was invited to deliver some sales training for some clients in Dubai. It was over three days and I trained over 60 people. Nothing unusual about that, but carting 60 sets of workbooks through the skies meant I had to take out with me 2 large suitcases, one completely filled with workbooks.

Naturally on my return journey I still had two large suitcases, again nothing odd there. But if you factor in that I was a businessman in a suit returning from a business trip in Dubai with two huge suitcases, it does start to look a little out of the ordinary.

The customs official at Heathrow airport thought so too and beckoned me over as I passed through customs. Here comes the suitcase search I thought, thinking about missing my train home.

He began by asking me some odd questions:

"How are you today sir?" – Fine.

"Do these suitcases belong to you?" – Yes (obviously, since I was carrying them).

"Have you been to Dubai on business?" – Yes (obviously really since I was in a suit).

"Was it warm out there?" – Yes (obviously again, it's always warm in Dubai).

I soon figured what he was doing. He was observing me closely, looking at my physiology – body language, facial expressions – he was observing my signals when I said the word "yes". I knew what he was going to do next. Do the same thing with the word "no".

"Did you manage to get any sleep?" – No (obviously – it was a daytime flight of only 6 hours).

"Have you been doing any dangerous sports in Dubai sir?" – No (good odds that most business meetings in Dubai don't involve bungee jumping).

"Do you have anything in those cases, that shouldn't be in there?" – No (this was the truth).

"Off you go then sir, and sorry to trouble you". And I left.

You see he had calibrated my physiology for when I said no and was telling the truth. The body doesn't lie, there's a tell for everything and he found it for the word "no" and didn't even bother to search the case. Clever man.

The police do this, so do barristers in court. I do it with my three children and I know when they're lying.

Remember, physiology, there's always a tell for everything you do.

Thankfully I managed to catch my train home, it was a long arduous journey and I was keen to get the train so thank you NLP calibration for helping me do this.

Precision Questions to Handle Reservations

The Meta Model

When people talk, they delete a great amount of material, they generalise in their speech and use plenty of distortions. It is the nature of language that not everything is said. Much of our language is nothing more than wild generalisations and assumptions.

If people tell you with precision what specifically is bothering them, and if you can find out what they want instead, you can deal with it. If they use vague phrases and generalisations, you're just lost in the mental fog. The key to effective communication is to break through that fog.

The NLP Meta Model helps enormously here, but it is shrouded in complex terms, which I've simplified.

The Response "Why" Gets You

What's the usual response to the customer saying?

This in turn produces all the reasons why the customer doesn't want to buy. They're on the defensive.

By being clever with the response, you can maintain rapport and build the conversation to achieve a win-win. Here's some ways of probing.

The purpose of precision in language is to find out as much useful information as possible. One way to deal with mental fog is the precision model. This will allow you to use new styles of questions that will allow you to dig deeper without breaking rapport.

Precision Questions

Missing information	As the name suggests, these can be statements where some meaning or information has been deleted.

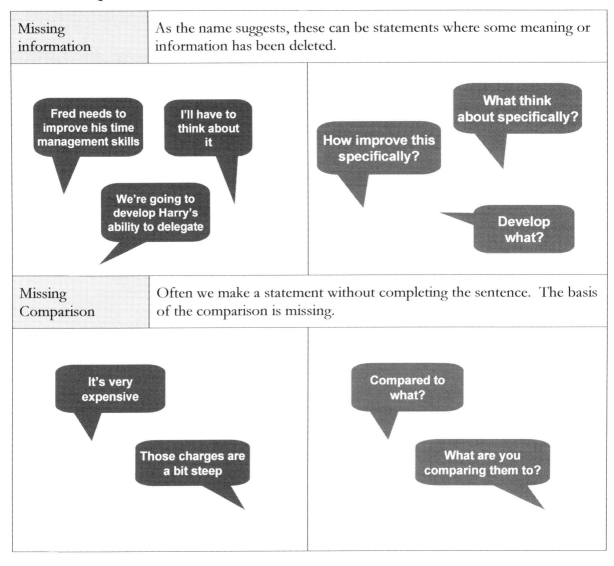

Missing Comparison	Often we make a statement without completing the sentence. The basis of the comparison is missing.

Sweeping statements	This kind of statement occurs when people express an opinion as if it were truth. On examination it's an opinion. Often these value judgements evolve from the past.

 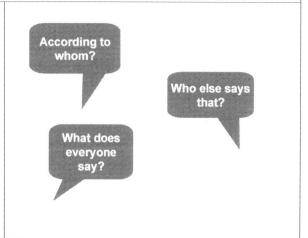

Brick walls	These consist of words such as no one, everyone, never, always, all, nothing. The speaker has generalised specific experiences to make them true in all circumstances.

 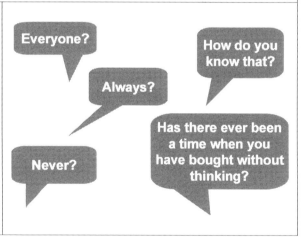

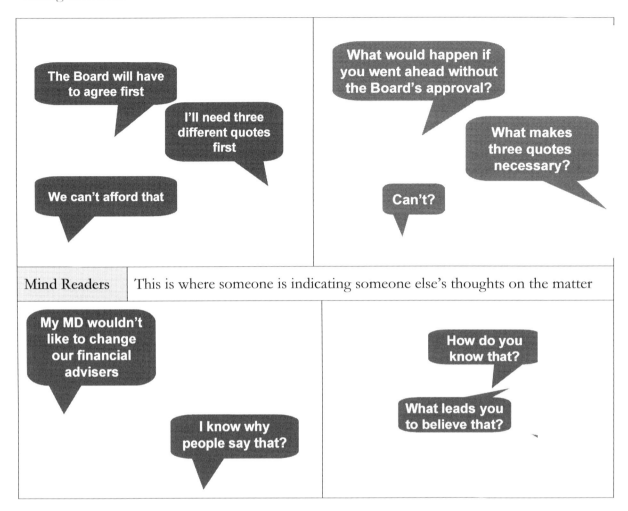

Mind Readers | This is where someone is indicating someone else's thoughts on the matter

Beware the Rising Tone

Christmas is almost here and I'm so excited. I love Christmas so here's a smashing little tip which will be very useful if you ever ask questions when selling. And let's face it, who doesn't.

"It's called early teenage talk, Paul".

That was the response from a teenage expert after I asked about the irritating habit I've noticed my teenage son using when talking to his friends. "It's called teenage talk".

So what is this annoying habit that causes this grumpy old man to moan?

It's the constant rising tonality of every sentence that my son uses. His sentences start normal and then his voice rises at the end of the phrase or sentence. This continues for hours. Have you noticed it from others?

Now it's not going to harm anyone and I should move on to worry about more important things but it actually is important in sales. More than people think.

We all know that communication is more than just the words chosen. Plenty of research carried out over the last 30 years shows that face to face communication consists of three parts – the words, the way you say them and the body language that's used to launch the words. The tone of the voice has a remarkable influence on the meaning, more that we think.

Straightforward really. A flat tone tells you that the sentence is just a statement. A falling tone indicates a command and a rising sentence says there is a question here.

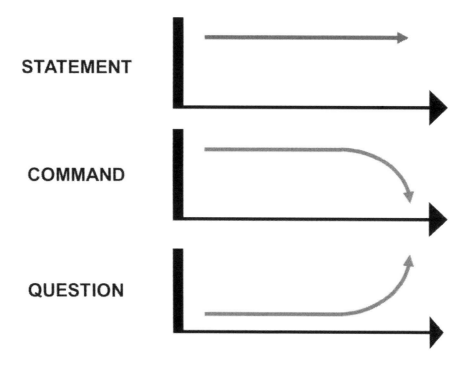

Try it now. Say something like, "It's time to go to bed". Say it with a flat, falling and then a rising tone and listen to the impact. It really works doesn't it?

Now this little gem has a couple of practical sales uses. I like practical don't you?

Firstly when asking question to find out your customer's needs and pains, make the questioning more palatable for them, by raising your tone a little. This makes the question you ask much more pleasing to the ear and you'll never be accused of interrogating your customer.

Secondly, when you want your customer to do something, drop your tone a little but only just a little. "So Bob, you're happy to go ahead with the paperwork then?" It's sounds like a question but the customer will accept it as a command. A little hypnotic maybe but your customer will do as you wish, and fill in the paperwork to seal the sale.

Now why do teenagers talk with rising tones on every sentence? I've no idea. It's probably something to do with wanting a reaction to everything they say and so raising the tone in your sentence makes it sound like a question.

Or just maybe it's just one of those things my teenage son does to irritate a grumpy old man like me.

Why Do We Have Eyebrows?

It's not to keep out sweat from your brow or to make us look pretty.

It's to help the human be congruent with their message. You see, when we talk our eyebrows have an uncanny way of backing up what we say. For example if you're asking a question, your eyebrows rise and if you look perplexed, I bet your eyebrows move inwards.

In the same way your voice tone varies. Let me explain how you can use this little known technique to help you close more sales.

You see if you ask a question, your voice tone rises. It's natural, is what we expect and helps the person you are talking to accept the question as genuine.

If you make a command or an instruction, your voice tone falls. It has depth and congruence to the command and people will obey.

There's two uses.

To lead a close say something like "So do you think this is the right package for you?" Yes it's a question but if you say it with a falling tone, the command tone, then the customer will accept it as a command and will hypnotically say yes.

Here's the second idea. To make a statement sound doubtful, say something like "The competition is strong in this area". Say it with a rising tone and the customer will think this is a question and will doubt the statement, which is what you want.

Clever eh? Do experiment, have fun and remember if you are genuine and have morals and integrity then feel free to use these hypnotic selling techniques. You are, aren't you?

Tailoring Your Selling With NLP

The Keys to Influencing

Have you ever delivered a motivational message to a group of people or given a speech to a group of factory floor workers? You can't help noticing how people react differently to your message. Some are spellbound, whereas others are not interested at all.

Have you ever told a good joke to a group of people – one person howls with laughter, whereas the others don't move a muscle.

The question is why do people react so differently to the same message? Why do some people see the glass as half empty and some as half full?

Everybody sorts their experiences in terms of what is important for them. NLP calls these meta programs – they are powerful internal patterns that help us to come to decisions. We reveal our methods for coming to decisions as we speak.

Towards And Away From

A couple of years ago I injured my back. After a short rest period, my doctor recommended that I built up my back muscles to prevent the problem from happening again. My job is sedentary with many hours sitting in a car travelling the length and breadth of the UK. So as not to endure the excruciating pain again, I joined my local gym and was soon shown an exercise routine that would strengthen my back.

Talking to some members during the exercises, it appears that people are motivated to exercise in one of two ways. Some are like me; they are fearful of the consequences of not exercising and some just enjoy the pleasure they get from exercising. It makes them feel good, especially when the endorphins are released into their brains.

Your customer will have a dominant preference of either moving away from things or towards things. The pensions your customers are arranging for their clients may mean that they can achieve their long-term objective of retiring comfortably and financially secure. Or it could mean that they're not going to be the same as their grandfather -- stuck on the fifth floor of the council tower block surviving on the state pension.

Internal And External

How do you know when you've done a good job? Is it when:

- You hear people saying what a good job you've done

- You feel good inside
- You've met the standards you've set yourself
- You can honestly say to yourself that you've done a good job

If you need external approval, such as getting more praise, then you probably have an external frame of reference.

For others, the proof comes from inside. The painter and decorator who has just spent three days in the blazing summer sun painting the outside of a large four bedroom detached house, stands back to admire his work and sees a slight blemish. Twenty minutes later, it's sorted and he once again stands back to admire his professional job. "Uhm" he thinks, "just perfect".

The situation will determine whether you are internal or external, but like many of these decision methods, everyone will have a dominant mode. For example, you finally finished cutting the grass – it's a lovely job and you know it. You don't need anyone else to say so – after all, you've cut the same grass umpteen times. The following weekend, after a day's blood, sweat and tears, you manage to tidy up your garage, which hasn't been touched for over two years. It looks good and you're happy, but you don't do this job often so some external praise will not go amiss.

We said earlier that careful questioning and active listening will elicit your customer's decision methods. Some questions which could work for external and internal are:

Similarities Versus Differences

Look at these shapes. Please describe their relationship to each other.

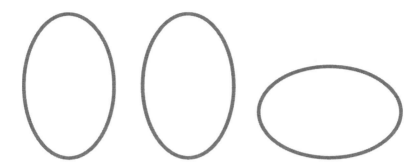

What do you notice? Do you notice in what ways they are similar i.e. they are all oval shapes? Do you notice that two are upright and one is lying down? Do you look for the sameness in things or do you look for what is different?

When you see a new car that's just been advertised on the TV for real on the motorway, what do you look for? Do you look for the radical new design of the vehicle or do you notice that the car is quite similar to the 311xsi?

Similarities deciders are constantly looking to compare any new information or communication with what they know. They match it up with something they are familiar with in order to judge it. When selling to someone like this you have to establish the favourable references and make sure that you compare with these.

For example, recently I was dealing with a potential client who was interested in presentation skills training for his senior salespeople since they were increasingly being called to deliver large presentations to large audiences. As we discussed his needs, he would constantly compare his requirements to a course he attended many years ago when he first started in the industry. He was seeking similarities to this course. I probed to find out what it was he liked about that course and these became the benefits of our training course.

Video was a feature and this became a major advantage of our course. "Each of the delegates will be given the opportunity to have their presentation recorded," I added, "and they'll get personal coaching on their performance". Business related topics which form the basis of role plays was a feature. "Our course," I continued, "this requires that delegates bring with them a prepared presentation for a real life talk that they are going to give over the next few months. This presentation will be used during the training." He bought the training.

Differences people are easily spotted as they respond with the opposite view to what you are saying. If the client in the example above were a differences person, then I would have stressed how unique our course was to the competition, what made it stand out from the crowd.

Big Chunk Small Chunk

I vividly remember attending a team building course a few years ago. I was put into a team of four people and we were given a large bag of children's play dough, some washable paint, straws, twigs, a plastic mat and many other "Blue Peter" style items. There were about ten other similar sized teams in a very large hall.

Our job, for a few hours, was to build a model island on the floor and decide on the overall strategy for this new community.

Typically with these team games, it took about twenty minutes to begin to 'gel' with the other members. We slapped the play dough on the mat and began to mould our island, painting forests and creating ports for supplies, helicopter landing pads, defence areas with anti aircraft guns (we were all boys!) etc.

Two of the guys in the group lost interest in this creative side of constructing the island and began to talk about our role in the sea of islands in the big room. What were we going to do to be able to trade, what goods could we export, how would we be ruled, what is the island's purpose? Meanwhile, the other chap and I had great fun filling in the detail of our island, creating housing complexes, deep water reservoirs for fresh water, road systems etc.

We'd slipped into our natural roles of big and small picture people and got the job done.

The big chunk person likes to look at the big picture in order to get a clear impression before making a decision. A small chunk person will want all the details and scrutinise the figures with a fine toothcomb.

Manchester United and the Big Picture

It was our first time going to Old Trafford even though I've supported my team since I was 7 years old. But our tickets were miles up in the north east stand and I said to my two boys that we're not going to able to see much, but at least there'll be a good atmosphere.

How wrong was I?

Because the stands are virtually vertical, we could see everything just by looking down at the pitch. I saw the defence positions when we were attacking. I saw the away fans in the corner making so much noise. I could see the linesmen running up and down the line and appreciated how complex their role is.

I had the whole scene in front of me. If I'd been watching on TV, yes I would've been closer to the play, but I would not know what was going on around the immediate vicinity of the ball and I would be at the behest of the cameraman.

In sales, we do need to have a firm eye on the bigger picture, especially if we want to cross or up sell. I prefer to call this upgrading – it's far more consumer friendly. By seeing the bigger picture, we can gauge the enormity of the problem the customer is struggling to solve, and see if there are other issues at play. Who makes the decisions, who else is involved?

How do we do this? Like every aspect of selling, it's about the question you ask.

- What's this a part of?
- What's the bigger picture behind this issue?
- What's the project that surrounds this?
- Is this part of a bigger issue?

I never knew that linesmen only run half a pitch. They only occupy one half each and work together to cover the pitch. I always wondered why they were so much quicker than the players.

The Stepping Stone Routine for Client Referrals

Stepping stones are great things to cross streams with. They make a large distance shrink because you're taking small steps rather than one big lunge.

Likewise when asking for client referrals, literally coming out with the ask is often too big, so adopt the stepping stone technique.

Let me explain.

As soon as your customer enjoys your value, whatever that is, ask them for some feedback, so they can verbally tell you about the value.

A little later on, you might want to ask if they wouldn't mind giving you a testimonial, maybe for your website or LinkedIn profile. A slightly bigger ask, but easily done especially if you provide the words or template.

Shortly afterwards, you might want them to work with you on a case study which highlights the benefits and value you were able to provide.

Finally, you can then ask them for a referral, i.e. an introduction to someone in their network who also might benefit from your value.

It's stepping stones and the theory comes from the principle of influencing called commitment and consistency...but I prefer to call it stepping stones.

Latch Onto your Customer's Buying Sequence

We all know that our customers are in control of buying these days. And that's all buyers, be they consumers or company buyers. They have the internet to do their product research and don't rely on salespeople to help them buy, many don't even want to be near one.

Commodity salespeople should move on but if your product is not a commodity, then you must evolve. We're no longer product pushers; we must consult and help the customer to buy by providing a bespoke and tailored solution.

If we're now consulting, it's essential that we tailor our sales message to their way of buying – to latch onto their way of buying. Here's how using some ingredients from NLP can work really well in selling.

Listen for how they make decisions.

These essential keys can help you enormously when communicating, asking the right questions, tailoring your message and presenting. They're known as meta-programmes in NLP but you don' need to call them that – I call it the graphic equaliser.

I use the following imaginary checklist, our role is to listen very carefully to the customer and place them along the line where they are for the context of buying:

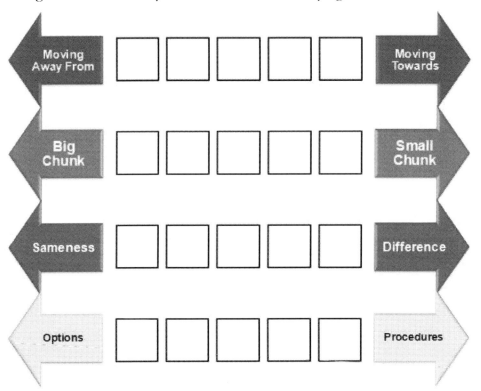

Here's ways you can assess them just by watching for body language.

Towards leaning people will tend to lean forward, watch their spine carefully since they'll be slightly forward. Away from people will be leaning backwards.

Big chunk people will make big sweeping gestures whereas small chunk people will make small gestures or none at all. Do listen to what they say as well.

You can spot procedures people because their gestures are always indicating a sequence or steps. Options people are all over the place.

Check for values, criteria and rules.

These are essential if you want to be able to tailor your solution to suit them. Ask questions such as:

- What is it you want in your (mortgage)?
- What's important to you in your new (mortgage)?
- What does a (mortgage) mean to you?

Elicit their values, rules and buying criteria from these questions.

Discover their Buying and Decision Strategy

This builds on the work we've done before on NLP's decision styles – visual – kinaesthetic – auditory and digital. We're looking for a sequence and a final decision strategy.

Let me give you an example.

The last major purchase I made was my Microsoft Band. Firstly I like to look around on websites at pictures of the product, and at the same time checking all the technical details and features to weigh up the product in my mind. Finally I'll buy when it feels right bearing in mind all my research or when the price dropped, which it did.

So my buying strategy is V – D – K or visual, digital and finally kino to make a decision.

On my seminars I talk about the story of our cleaner – Tracey – and how I'm in awe at how she worked so diligently, so I asked her a series of questions to elicit her cleaning sequence.

"When you enter a room, what do you do first?"

"What's the very first step you take?"

"And what do you do next?"

"And how do you decide it's done?"

It turns out that Tracey walks into a room that needs cleaning. She immediately compares in her minds' eye the picture she has of the room perfectly cleaned. She looks at the room facing her and then realises what needs to be done.

This sequence involves two visuals – one internal and one external – called Vi and Ve.

This sequence loops as she moves around the room.

"What keeps you motivated, Tracey?"

"I say to myself that this room will soon be looking a whole lot better."

Auditory internal – Ai

"And when will you know it's done?"

"It looks right and as it should be and I just know I've done a good job."

More Ve and a final kinaesthetic internal feeling – Ki.

So Tracey's sequence is Vi – Ve – Ai – Ki.

Back to selling, let's look at another example so you can see how this might be useful for, say a car salesperson. People do buy cars online nowadays but for the time being, we still have car showrooms and salespeople.

I bought a car last week for my eldest son, it was his money but he wanted me to buy it for him, as he thought I would negotiate a good deal. How did I buy the car?

Firstly I looked online, on YouTube and manufacturers' websites – my Ve again – visual external. This time I then looked around at reviews, what others were saying about the cars and the dealers. This is auditory external essentially since I read the reviews out loud – Ae.

Then we reached the stage of driving and you can't do this yet online, so an appointment was made with the dealer. After a brief phone call the VW garage arranged to send one over for us to drive for a day or two. This satisfied my kinaesthetic or touch need – Ke.

Finally we made an appointment to finalise things and sat down with the salesperson – Arif. He was new to the business, nice chap, but rather new. He was following his script bless him, and it wasn't mine. My buying sequence had two more elements – firstly the deal, I wanted a good deal on price and other accessories and was about to enter into negotiation.

But Arif was trying to sell me gap insurance and go through the paperwork. I wasn't ready for this. So I grabbed his paper and went digital on him, I wanted a logical and fair outcome on price. On the paper I wrote down all the variables that makes up a car purchase:

- Price
- Tank of fuel
- Mats

- Warranty
- Service Plan
- Tax

And we started to negotiate – you see I negotiate using a digital strategy nothing else – D.

The manager was involved as the negotiation ensued and eventually a win:win was achieved. I felt good inside and felt that the time was right to pay the money.

My final Ki.

So my sequence – Ve – Ae – Ke – D – Ki.

Looking at models, reading reviews, feeling the product, getting a deal and finally feeling just right.

If Arif had asked me some questions such as:

"What did you do first on your buying journey?"

"What then?"

"What next?"

"And when you arrived here, what other steps are important to you to help you make a decision?"

Then he could have tailored his selling to me in the same way you can for your next customer.

By the way, I got a small reduction on price after all, it was priced to sell, mats, a full tank of fuel and a year's service plan. Plus a year's tax.

Discovering Client Buying Strategies

The good thing about strategies is that if you take someone back to the time they made a good buying decision in the past, they will run through their buying strategy again for you. So all you need to do is ask.

You can detect their strategy in two ways:

Firstly they will verbally tell you the process they went through, during which you can pick up their strategy from the predicates they use.

An example.

For instance, if we used the example above, they might say:

and it felt like the right choice for me

Kinaesthetic

Secondly, they will run through the strategy internally so their eyes will mark out the strategy for you.

The great thing about eye accessing patterns is that even if your client doesn't verbally give you the answer, they will always give you their eye accessing patterns.

A Good Space

End of school holidays, Sunday lunch, Archer household, deepest Gloucestershire.

"So Bethan, are you looking forward to starting in big school next week?"

"Yes, Daddy lots, I'm looking forward to seeing all my old friends and making new friends."

"That's lovely Boo, that's a wonderful thought you have in your head. You hold onto that."

"I will Daddy, I will, how can I do that Daddy?"

"I'll show you how. Before that show me where that wonderful thought is…point to it, baby."

"It's there Daddy."

Bethan pointed upwards to her right. And I'd discovered where my daughter puts her good feelings.

Now this is particularly useful to me now, but let me explain first why.

You see people put things in places in their heads, it's how folk roll. Ask them a question to allow them to look in their good place direction, Bethan's was front right slightly upwards. This allows you to influence them hypnotically in a number of ways.

For example, if you want them to feel good about your sales proposal, then place it in their line where good thoughts happen. Easy.

Or move into a position where they see you in their "happy" place and your message will be joyfully received.

And you could even find out their bad space and talk about the competition whilst in that space.

Useful, don't you think?

And for Boo, she's aware of her good place and can put all her thinking there especially going to big school and meeting all her new friends. We just have to be ready for the real impact of big school with 2,500 pupils in one building. Good job I know where her good place is.

Calibrating your Customer

On holiday this year I read the book "Fifty Shades of Grey" just to see what all the fuss was about and so I could keep up with conversations about the characters Christian and Anastasia.

Christian, the hero of the book, is particularly good at observing people, especially facial expressions and signals. He notices early on that Anastasia bites her lower lip when she meets him. He finds this enticing.

Don't worry this is not an X rated article. Read on and I'll explain how this can help you in sales and coaching.

Not a lot of people know this but when someone gets interested, energised, in an emotional state of excited motivation, blood rushes to the lower lip slightly engorging it. You can see this because the lines disappear as the lip fills.

Now if your customer did this, it's a great buying signal. Christian read it as such too. I'd be wanting to close my customer and ask for the business at this point.

This is one example of calibrating your customer and observing those tiny changes in the face. The reddening of cheeks, the eyes, the lips, furrowed brow. Seasoned salespeople read these signs instinctively, others must learn to.

When you meet your customer, calibrate their face and then spot the subtle changes and act upon them. Reading body language is not so important as being able to read the face.

With the rise of Skype based video communications and Google Hangouts, we should become acutely aware of these facial signals.

It's a good book by the way but make sure you read it on your Kindle – that way no one knows what you're reading. After all, a man shouldn't be seen reading that!

NLP and Modelling Top Performers

Without the ability to model people, NLP would never have been created. Essentially NLP is a collection of tools that have been extracted from top performing people in many different fields and it continues to evolve.

Many years ago, John Grinder and Richard Bandler set out to discover how great people became great at what they did.

Bandler was a computer modeller. He wanted to teach a computer to do what a human being could do. He studied very carefully the work of Virginia Satir and Milton H Erickson, who are generally accepted these days as introducing hypnosis into the medical field.

One of the things they discovered was that if you asked people directly how they did something, they may give a brief explanation of what they thought they did, but that it was mostly instinctive.

So, at its simplest, NLP Behavioural Modelling is the study of what accounts for the results that people achieve. In other words what are the thoughts, behaviours, skills, beliefs, values, and other attitudinal qualities that they use to do what they do.

And this is why I've included modelling in my NLP in Sales book since it can and has been used to model the behaviours of top performing salespeople so you can give the results to others in your coaching and training. I'm going to show you the process, then talk you through a case study which I carried out last year for a large organisation looking to recruit and train a new salesforce.

So how do you model? Here's the process:

How to Model Behaviour

At its simplest:

1. Become interested and curious
2. Create rapport
3. Ask questions to elicit supporting beliefs, criteria, strategies and then behaviours
4. Listen and check your understanding of what they describe
5. Pay particular attention to their non-verbal communication
6. Try to move to a second or third perceptual position – in their shoes not yours
7. Check your understanding periodically

The first 2 we've talked about before as the last 4, but it's point number 3 that I'd like to show you some more.

| Enabling beliefs | Motivating beliefs | Primary strategy | Secondary strategy | External behaviour | Ability |

Your questioning needs to elicit both enabling and motivating beliefs. I feel this is the vital part of modelling as much of a salesperson's ability comes down to what they believe in. Then we're into strategies.

Now don't confuse actions or behaviours with strategies in NLP. If we want to create a skill and just concentrate on the behaviour, ignoring the thoughts, then we are likely to only have half of the story, getting poor results.

The essence of NLP strategies is that we all use a sequence of internal representations or thinking styles in order to accomplish things in life. These are our thoughts, our thinking at that time. It's the thinking that triggers the behaviour.

On my NLP Master Programme I was asked to be modelled by another student who asked me what particular skill I have. That was a difficult question to answer until I realised that I'm quite good at completing things and never give up until I'm successful – being tenacious.

So she set about modelling me on this. The belief system was interesting – I believe in succeeding against all odds, being the underdog who can rise and be successful, that anything is possible if you keep at it and that by changing your approach you will get success.

My strategies were interesting. I'm very towards the outcome, quite small chunk in detail and definitely more internal than external which gives me the capability of providing my own drive and energy.

My strategy was this – Ai – Vi – Ai – D – Vi - Ki.

Talking to myself about the goal in mind, then visualising the outcome of achieving the task i.e. the reward. Telling myself to try option A. If this fails try option B, a sequence of options until I get the success, a quick look at the goal I set to see if they compare and then a warm kino feeling to know I've been successful.

This drove my behaviour which gave me the ability.

In June 2014 I was commissioned to design the training and development programme for a whole new sales team of over 250 recruits who were going to be brought into the team over the next 12 months. They had around 15 existing salespeople who were providing the service where I could choose my SME – subject matter expert.

The company is a large retail bank providing mortgage advice to customers but using video technology rather than being face to face, so the training of the new salespeople had to prepare them for this. As part of the curriculum preparation, I modelled a couple of their best performers.

Here's the outcome:

Belief Template

Enabling beliefs

- Progression, getting on, rising up the ladder was evident
- The strongest enabling belief was to do a good job for the customer, the mortgage is a life changing event for people and we are emboldened to get it right
- A yearning to foster a relationship with the customer which is true and honest
- People buy people and this belief transfers itself to the video connection. The trust building manifested as a behaviour
- An enjoyment of being with people

Motivating beliefs

- To get it right, a correct recommendation. This away from strategy seems a strong driver amongst the consultants which was possibly given to them by the team manager.

Primary Strategy

- Ai – Ki – Ae – Listen to the customer, build trust by hearing for common ground seeking to be trusted followed by a jovial nature in what they say.
- To build trust – commonality, intention and competence – is a paramount strategy and the sellers find a way with the equipment they use. Internally represented to listen well rather than do all the talking.
- The use of humour and examples was evident.
- Being an expert and a trusted adviser, one who will get it right. An away strategy here.
- A strong towards motivating belief in giving a correct recommendation is taken to its limit, even overdoing it, as the primary directive is giving the right advice. They have

a strategy taken from IFAs where fees empowered them to be responsible for their advice.

External Behaviour

- Trust building
- Listening to level 3 the majority of the time, an acute awareness of the customer on the screen with a very capable peripheral vision
- Humour and the use of past own experience to illustrate
- Diligent and an attention to detail driven by small chunk style

Ability

- To create a relationship with the customer of trust, using the video equipment and to coach the customer to achieve the most correct advice possible surrounding their mortgage and protection needs.

33452607R00099

Printed in Great Britain
by Amazon